THE LOGIC OF
STRATEGIC PLANNING

The Little, Brown Series in
Strategy and Policy

Charles E. Summer,
Editor

THE LOGIC OF
STRATEGIC
PLANNING

John H. Grant
William R. King

University of Pittsburgh

Little, Brown and Company

Boston   Toronto

TO
LAURA & DEREK
AND SUZAN

Library of Congress Catalog Card No. 81-82107

ISBN 0-316-324078

9 8 7 6 5 4 3 2 1

ALP

Published simultaneously in Canada
by Little, Brown & Company (Canada) Limited

Printed in the United States of America

page 68: Reprinted by permission from Harold W. Fox, "Framework for Functional Coordination," *Atlanta Economic Review*, November–December, 1973, p. 10.

page 143: Reprinted by permission of the Institute for Management Science. George W. Gershefski, "Corporate Models: The State of the Art," *Management Science* Vol. 16, No. 6, Copyright © February 1970, p. B-309.

FOREWORD

THE LITTLE, BROWN SERIES IN STRATEGY AND POLICY consists of a group
of books addressed to problems of increasing importance to large
complex organizations in business and government. Existing books in
such fields as organizational behavior, management, administrative
behavior, and operations research have dealt with decision making
inside organizations, and with human behavior inside organizations.
Existing books in political science have dealt with discrete, partial,
and piecemeal decision making as it occurs in the political arena. But
as industrial societies become ever larger and more complex, there is
a general feeling in both academic and practicing management circles that "something is missing."

In a purely scientific (descriptive) sense, there is a great deal of
action taking place at the very highest levels in corporations and
government agencies that these micro (internal) approaches have not
explained. General managers, policy makers, strategists, top managers, or whatever you wish, are in fact making decisions and engaging
in forms of human leadership which are not explainable by theories of
decision making that apply at the middle and lower levels of organizations, and which are not explainable by theories of leadership in
small face-to-face groups. One thing that "is missing" is a description
of how top level managers go about two things: decision making and
human leadership. Books in this series will show that the making of
global, gestalt, holistic, comprehensive decisions that relate the entire
organization to the society around it is a far different matter from the
more meticulous, analytical, fragmentary decision making that must
occur later as strategic decisions are implemented. Scientific analysis,
from cost-benefit analysis to market research, has its place in policy
making but only after the strategic decisions have found, identified,
and formulated the global problem. Though policy analysis has an
important place in strategy formulation and implementation, it is

precisely because of the importance of problem finding and problem focusing that the terms "strategy formulation" and "policy formulation" have come to be commonly used in the literature. Books in this series will indeed recognize the importance of science and policy analysis in the whole process of strategic decision making. Most of them include tools, techniques, and analytical methods that are relevant to strategy and policy formulation. But these methods of science interact with conceptual logic and even with ethical principles. Only in ineffective practice would they precede a definition of the strategic problem that, from society's viewpoint, requires focus and attention.

A second thing that "is missing" in much of the social science literature is a normative approach. Social scientists are quite right in trying to discover how managers *do* behave rather than how they *should* or *ought to* behave. In this respect they are obeying the canons of science. But that leaves a vital question demanded by society and by professional managers unanswered: How ought managers behave in relation to the needs of society? Society profoundly depends upon large productive organizations, from medical clinics that meet the demand for human health to commercial banks that meet the demand for loans to build shelter. Not only does the standard of living in society depend upon technical and economic leadership; the cultural welfare of society depends upon cultural leadership — a leadership which takes into account the intangible values (e.g., freedom, justice, ecological balance, fraternity) of society. These are matters that most social scientists have either deliberately ignored or perhaps hidden in a mass of factual techniques and assumptions.

For example, "good" science of organizational behavior explains how supervisors should act in order to promote the self-actualization and growth of human beings. "Good" accounting, finance, and operations research show how managers should rationalize resources to achieve efficient production and achieve a level of minimum waste of resources. But we have little "good" strategy and policy literature that shows how top level managers either *do* or *ought to* go about 1) defining and formulating the standard of living missions of society, 2) adjusting the organization's production system so that both standard of living and cultural values are taken into account, 3) exercising a kind of leadership that is acceptable to the organization and to society, and 4) insuring the health of the corporation or the government agency itself so that it survives and continues to serve society.

In general, these are the problems that the field of strategy and policy study. As we move into the last part of the twentieth century, in which industrial society is forced to depend on ever larger and more complex organizations to satisfy its needs, this field will become more important. The first three books in the series approach these problems in different ways. But they are similar in that they study the actions and behavior of top managers, strategists, and policy makers. They focus on the global management of total organizations as they relate to their social environments. They study this behavior in two ways: how strategists *do* behave and how managers *ought to* or *might* behave in order to be more effective in solving strategic problems.

In this last respect, much of the literature that deals with top level managerial behavior is critical. It shows the malfunctioning of large organizations when they fail to serve society. Or it shows the abuses which top leaders have inflicted on organizations, society, and the public trust. Though such malfunctioning and such abuses do indeed exist in society, there is also a great deal of effective organizational behavior and effective strategic leadership which occurs. These books concentrate on this neglected side of organizational and leader performance.

Finally, all three books view strategy formulation, policy making, and leadership as a dynamic process, in which general managers interact with social forces inside and outside the organization in a *never ending process of organizational development and change.* They do not depict organizations as static, mechanistic forms that exhibit the negative side of bureaucracy. Nor do they view strategists as persons who mastermind some rational plan to satisfy needs for status, technical elegance or psychological dominance. Rather, strategists are continually coping, sometimes in a comprehensive and logical (stable) way and sometimes in a partially logical (unstable) way, to steer big organizations through their evolutionary life cycles in ways that satisfy social demands.

Of the first three series books, two are addressed primarily to strategy and policy in business corporations, while one focuses on these problems in both business corporations and government agencies. Forthcoming books are committed to adding to knowledge both in the private sector and in the government sector.

John H. Grant and William R. King, in *The Logic of Strategic Planning*, give an overview of strategic planning as it is done in both single-product and multi-product enterprises. They show problem formulation as a conceptual and logical process (to define the company's product and market mission) and a collateral analytical process (i.e., they give tools and techniques for analyzing product portfolios and for investigating financial, marketing, and human resources). This book is one of the most complete summaries of "the state of the art" of strategic planning as it is accomplished in business corporations.

In *Strategies for Diversification and Change*, Milton Leontiades covers existing descriptive models of how corporations progress from simple, one-product companies to very complex corporations serving many market constituencies. He focuses on diversification, by

vii

means of unrelated acquisitions, as the dominant current process of corporate development—a process where practice has thus far preceded theory. As I have in my book, he also stresses the long, evolutionary, trial and error development of the corporation. This is a process in which strategists interact with various constituencies in society to plot a path of growth. Both books are separated into two parts, the first descriptive (how corporations actually behave) and the second normative (some ways they might behave to better satisfy demands from constituencies). In the latter part of the book, as he applies a proposed growth path model, Leontiades shows that planners accomplish one other important thing as they match their planning systems to their overall strategic missions: they devise an organization network that somehow copes with the masses of information needed in strategic planning without causing an information overload on the organization or "future shock" to strategists.

Finally my own book, *Strategic Behavior in Business and Government*, as the title implies, shows that there is a great deal of strategic planning done in government in the United States but that much of this has gone unrecognized. The secretary of Health, Education and Welfare behaves in a way strikingly similar to the way the president of General Motors behaves when planning global, comprehensive strategies and when implementing them by an intricate rationalization of internal resources. Furthermore, the health or education industries in this country evolve their organization structures in very much the same way as companies in the electronics industry or the automobile industry evolve theirs. This is true of organizations which range from Hewlett Packard Corporation to Group Health Hospitals or the Boston Symphony Orchestra.

These three books are intended for use by students in advanced undergraduate courses and masters level courses in schools of business administration (all three books) and public administration (one book). They are also intended for use by professional executives in business and government who are engaged in the difficult but challenging work of strategic planning and policy formulation.

As time goes on, other books in the series will continue to focus on the strategic viewpoint. The field of strategy and policy will become more and more important as society demands of its leaders both a degree of stability and order and a degree of flexibility and disorder. Time will tell whether or not the giant organizations of today, managed in part by strategists and policy makers, can walk the difficult tightrope in a way that is acceptable to society.

Charles E. Summer
Series Editor

PREFACE

IN RECENT YEARS strategic planning has come to the forefront of corporate management. This book focuses attention on one important dimension of strategic planning—the set of logical processes and techniques that supports strategic decision making.

The plan of the book is straightforward. Chapter 1 presents the basic ideas of strategic planning which will be used throughout the book. Although the reader may already be familiar with many of these ideas, the scientific nature of strategic management makes careful definition of terminology necessary. Chapter 1 also discusses the underlying framework of concepts that provides the basis for the organization of the rest of the book.

Chapter 2 elaborates on this framework and shows how it may be adjusted to apply to either integrated or diversified firms. In doing this, the chapter demonstrates the philosophy on which the book is based—that there is no universally correct way to plan, but that there is a standard against which planning can be judged and from which new planning approaches can be derived. Thus the framework of Chapter 1 provides the standard that is adapted in Chapter 2 to the two major varieties of business firms.

Planning is a field in which concepts have been only partially tested and in which there is little validated theory. In such an area, one is either a disbeliever who shuns all aspects of the theory, a believer who operates strictly on faith, or a pragmatist who recognizes the value of some approaches along with their lack of universal validity and applicability. This book adopts the pragmatic view. The standards are proposed not because they are "correct" in an absolute sense, but rather because they have proved to be useful in and adaptable to a

ix

wide variety of circumstances and situations. The reader is invited to scrutinize each standard that is presented here, whether it is a conceptual framework, a particular technique of environmental analysis, or a measure to evaluate divisional performance, and to consider its applicability to the reader's own situation. In many instances, it will be found that a minor adaptation will make it useful. This concept of a standard against which planning processes and techniques can be tested and from which special-purpose adaptations can be derived is fundamental to the entire book.

Chapters 3 through 8 deal with one important aspect of the planning framework—the conduct of internal strategic analyses—in the context of a specific business. The business so analyzed might be either an integrated firm or a single division of a diversified firm. In Chapter 11, this study is then complemented with a treatment of the special problems that relate to the diversified firm as a whole, rather than the individual business units of which it is composed. Specifically, Chapter 3 discusses the overall internal strategic analyses that may be conducted as a preliminary step in the study of the business. Chapters 4, 5, 6, and 7 then deal with internal analyses that may be conducted in the finance, marketing, manufacturing, research and development, and human resources areas of the business. Chapter 8 discusses integrated and overall business unit analyses that are best performed after all of the functional area analyses are complete.

Chapters 9 and 10 discuss the environmental analysis aspect of the planning framework in terms of both process and technique. Distinctions are made among the internal, operating, and general environmental levels, as well as among the various uses of such analyses.

As noted previously, Chapter 11 then addresses the special problems of the diversified firm.

Finally, Chapter 12 addresses the organizational and process dimensions of planning. Clearly, a single chapter does not permit exhaustive treatment of these dimensions. However, the critical elements for the implementation of planning are considered.

Since our selection and footnoting of many of the cases used as illustrations throughout this book, the Intercollegiate Case Clearing House has been replaced administratively by HBS Case Services. Most of the referenced ICCH cases are still available with the same titles and file numbers from HBS Case Services, Boston, Massachusetts 02163 (617/495-6117).

We wish to express our appreciation to all of those who have helped us with this effort in various ways. Since a list of such individuals would be quite extensive, we shall note only a few of those whose direct efforts were of critical importance. Milton Johnson and Alex Greene, as successive editors, provided guidance and encouragement. Charles Summer, the editor of this series, not only suggested a helpful title, but also provided valuable and detailed comments and critiques. Sally Lifland and her associates at Lifland et al., Bookmakers, transformed the manuscript into text format with skill and patience. Our research assistants have helped with references and have stimulated many of the ideas herein. Richard Rumelt of UCLA reviewed the initial manuscript and provided useful guidance that improved the book. Finally, Olivia Harris and Esther Lattner typed all of the manuscripts, tolerated our intolerance, and generally made the manuscript preparation effort efficient and enjoyable.

In spite of the substantial assistance which we have received from others, responsibility for any limitations, omissions, or errors remains with us.

John H. Grant
William R. King

CONTENTS

PART I
STRATEGIC PLANNING IN
INTEGRATED AND DIVERSIFIED FIRMS   1

CHAPTER 1   **Strategic Planning: A Logical Framework
for Managing**   3
Strategy, Plans, and Strategic Planning Systems   4
The Need for Strategy, Plans, and an SPS   4
The Logical Framework for Effective Strategic Planning   7
Using the SPS Framework   12
Chapter Summary and Overview of the Book   14
Notes   14

CHAPTER 2   **Strategic Planning in Integrated
and Diversified Firms**   16
*The Nature of Strategy in Integrated and Diversified
Firms*   17
*Strategic Organizational Characteristics of Integrated and
Diversified Firms*   18
Strategic Planning in the Integrated Firm   23
*Strategic Planning in Multiple Market or Diversified
Firms*   29
Summary   34
Notes   34

PART II
STRATEGIC ANALYSIS AT
THE BUSINESS UNIT LEVEL   37

CHAPTER 3   **Overall Strategic Analysis**   39

xiii

Identifying and Employing Comparative Advantage and
   Distinctive Competence   40
Overall Competitive Strategy Analysis   42
Overall Strategic Position Assessment   44
Assessing a Business Unit's Prospects for Forward or
   Backward Integration   47
Summary   50
Notes   50

CHAPTER 4   **Financial Aspects of**
                Strategy Analysis   51
Product Line Profitability   51
Capacity Expansion Analysis   57
Tax Analyses   58
Return on Investment Analysis   59
Cash Flow Analysis   60
Summary   61
Notes   61

CHAPTER 5   **Marketing Aspects of**
                Strategy Analysis   62
Growth-Share Matrix Analysis   62
Market Segmentation and Product Line Analysis   64
Product Life Cycle Analysis   66
Distribution and Logistical Elements of Strategy Analysis   71
Summary   72
Notes   72

CHAPTER 6   **Manufacturing Aspects of**
                Strategy Analysis   73
Strategy Relevance of Quality, Perceived Quality,
   and Price   73
Comparative Cost Analyses   75
Experience Curve Analysis   76
Minimum Efficient Scale Facilities   79
Capacity Utilization Analyses for Strategy   80
Materials Management Considerations   81
Summary   83
Notes   83

CHAPTER 7   **Research and Development and Human Resources**
                Aspects of Strategy Analysis   85
R&D Components of Strategy   85
Human Resources Aspects of Strategy Analysis   93
Summary   96
Notes   97

CHAPTER 8   **Integrated Strategic Analyses**   99
  PIMS Analysis   99
  Other Integrated Strategic Analyses   102
  Summary   106
  Notes   107

PART III
STRATEGIC ENVIRONMENTAL ANALYSIS   109

CHAPTER 9   **Environmental Analysis**   111
  The Role of Environmental Analysis in Planning   111
  An Environmental Assessment Process   119
  Environmental Information Systems   124
  Summary   130
  Notes   130

CHAPTER 10   **Techniques for**
             Environmental Assessment   132
  Techniques for Assessing the Current Environment   132
  Techniques for Assessing the Future Environment   134
  Techniques for Evaluating Alternative Futures   142
  Summary   146
  Notes   146

PART IV
STRATEGIC PLANNING IN
THE DIVERSIFIED FIRM   149

CHAPTER 11   **Planning in Diversified Firms**   151
  Stakeholder Analysis of the Diversified Firm   151
  Concepts and Models of a Business Portfolio   153
  Strategic Management of Business Portfolios   156
  Strategic Acquisition and Divestment Analysis   165
  Summary   172
  Notes   173

PART V
ORGANIZATIONS AND SYSTEMS FOR
STRATEGIC PLANNING   177

CHAPTER 12   **Organizational Structure and Processes**
             for Strategic Management   179
  Strategy Formulation and Implementation in Integrated
    and Diversified Firms   179
  Strategic Structural Change   182
  Assignment and Development of Management   186
  Designing Organizational Systems   189

Contents

Summary   195
Notes   195

Author Index   199
Subject Index   202

THE LOGIC OF
STRATEGIC PLANNING

PART I

STRATEGIC PLANNING
IN INTEGRATED AND
DIVERSIFIED FIRMS

CHAPTER 1

Strategic Planning:
A Logical Framework
for Managing

IN RECENT YEARS organizational strategic planning has become increasingly exact, with more of the attributes of a true science. The strategic planning concepts that were developed and refined during the 1970s provide contemporary managers with a powerful set of tools with which to guide organizational behavior through external environments and to streamline internal operations.

With strategic planning, an organization prepares for its future. Of course, many of the daily decisions and actions taken by managers and administrators have consequences that will be realized only in the future, so in some sense all such activities involve preparation for the future. *Strategic planning, however, involves an organization's most basic and important choices—the choice of its mission, objectives, strategy, policies, programs, goals, and major resource allocations.* These strategic choices, taken together, will largely determine the organization's overall future, whereas individual managerial decisions, particularly if they are made within the guidelines of established organization strategy and policy, will merely influence one aspect of the future.

Strategic choices—those which affect the basic direction and operation of the organization—are made by all organizations. Sometimes they are made implicitly and sometimes even unknowingly, but inevitably they are made through the actions or inactions of an organization's managers.

Strategic planning is the organized process through which such strategic decisions can be systematically and rationally analyzed and made. Without such an organized process, the far-reaching impact of strategic decisions will probably not be foreseen.

Of course, even formal strategic planning is not always performed

3

as a totally systematic and logical process. Sometimes plans are based on irrational hopes for future success; sometimes they are based only on simple extrapolations of the past. The thesis of this book, however, is that over the long term *the most effective organizational strategic planning will be that which is founded on a systematic and logical base.*

Strategy, Plans, and Strategic Planning Systems

There is a semantics jungle that exists in the field of management. The same words are used by various writers to mean different things. Some preliminary definitions are therefore in order.

As used here, a *strategy* is a timed sequence of internally consistent and conditional resource allocation decisions that are designed to fulfill an organization's objectives.

The *internal consistency* in a strategy prescribes a clear general direction in which the organization is to pursue its objectives. For instance, a good product development strategy would prescribe such a specific direction if it offered a technically feasible solution to needs of customers who were valued by the firm and who were willing to pay a price which would yield a satisfactory economic return.

A *strategic planning system* (SPS) is a set of interrelated organizational task definitions and procedures for seeing that pertinent information is obtained, forecasts are made, and strategy choices are addressed in an integrated, internally consistent, and timely fashion.

Plans are the documentary evidence that an SPS has functioned to produce a well-conceived strategy. They provide the reference point for the continuing evaluation of progress toward goals and for the re-examination of strategy. Plans reflect the outputs of a strategic planning system—the organization's chosen mission, objectives, and strategy.

The Need for Strategy, Plans, and an SPS

All organizations have a strategy—a general direction in which they are moving—but not all have plans and a strategic planning system.[1] Thus, the need for an explicit strategy, plans, and an SPS must be demonstrated.

4

The Importance of an Explicit Strategy

The desirability of an integrated and explicit strategy is obvious if one considers the only alternatives. If there is no strategy, or if the strategy is only implicit, a complex organization involving many different decisions and decision makers will be led toward making a series of unrelated choices in response to the exigencies of many different moments. Such strategic choices are usually not synergistic (mutually reinforcing), and they may even be contradictory. The lack of an overall strategy at the national level in the United States has created such a situation. The federal government simultaneously funds tobacco growing and cancer prevention, even though the two are known to be contradictory. This occurs because choices have been made independently to achieve different objectives which are, to some degree, in conflict.

Consciously selected strategies are internally consistent in that they allow mutually reinforcing relationships among the resources of a business. Strategies that are only implicit or are poorly devised will often not have this important characteristic. This will result in a weak link in the strategy that may cause the entire strategy to fail.

For instance, during the mid-1950s, the Crown Cork and Seal Company pursued a strategy that emphasized research and development (R&D) but neglected manufacturing efficiency and flexibility. As a result, the firm was unable to move new products into efficient manufacture fast enough to secure the higher profit margins that are usually available, at least temporarily, to an innovator. This and other strategic errors caused an erosion of profits that threatened the firm with bankruptcy, but new leadership implemented dramatic strategic changes quickly and successfully.[2]

On the other hand, the Design & Manufacturing Corporation's achievement of internal consistency in technological innovation, manufacturing processes, market segmentation, executive staffing, and capital structure provides an example of the way in which functional variables can be combined in a complementary fashion to provide technologically reliable, standardized, and low-cost products to a limited number of potentially strong customers in the home appliance industry.[3]

Sears, Roebuck & Company provides another example of the critical importance of internal consistency to strategic success. During much of the 1970s, the company was offering New York designers' high-fashion clothes from the same stores that were simultaneously discounting small appliances in an effort to fend off discounters, who were attacking Sears's customer base from the low end of the price

5

spectrum. Needless to say, it was difficult to attract customers from both expensive boutiques and low-price discount shops into the same store, regardless of its location. The logical inconsistencies in terms of product lines and company image led to some rather dramatic reordering of priorities and personnel during 1978 and 1979, but not until corporate performance had eroded significantly.[4]

In addition to having its own merits as an overall plan, a good internally consistent strategy also provides guidance for the many managers who must make tactical choices on a day-to-day basis. The existence and communication of a formal strategy ensures that these lower-level choices will be made in a fashion that is consistent with overall strategy. Without such formal guidance, middle managers are left to infer what the strategy is and what part their own choices might play in implementing it. Thus, the failure to develop and communicate a formal strategy leads to a series of guessing games that are not the stuff of which success is made.

The Need for Strategic Planning

Effective strategic planning—because it inherently involves foresight into an uncertain future—will probably always be carried out through a judicious mixture of reason and creativity, of analysis and judgment, of objective criteria and common sense. However, if the logical and systematic basis for planning is missing, it is unlikely that the planning will be effective over the long run. Thus, while there is much anecdotal evidence of casual and informal planning that somehow fortuitously resulted in success, there is also overwhelming evidence that such an approach cannot be relied on to do so. As examples, Theodore Levitt[5] has described many firms and industries that declined or disappeared in the face of a changing environment. The many examples include the failure of the movie industry to get into television when it had the resources and the opportunity to do so, and the railroads' failure to see their business as one of transportation rather than of railroading.

Many researchers[6] have studied the need for organizations to change their strategic posture in order to achieve greater recognition in the financial community, to turn around a deteriorating situation, or to more effectively respond to a changing environment. Chrysler Corporation, whose problems have been front-page news across the nation, was clearly unable to foresee and to respond to a changing market as quickly as did other firms. The relationship of this failure to the company's lack of planning can be surmised from a *Fortune* story:

It is somewhat strange that Cafiero, as president of the nɛ tenth-largest industrial organization, felt the need to seek advice of friends at companies like I.T.T. and General Foods in drawing up Chrysler's first long-term, company-wide plans.[7]

Antiplanners might say that these failures may not have been avoided through logical planning.[8] This is certainly true. Since these changing business environments were foreseeable, however, it is likely that a systematic and logical plan would have allowed the companies involved to detect and assess these changes, whereas uncoordinated individual insights did not.

This assertion recognizes that the environmental changes that have led to the demise of industries and firms are complex and difficult to assess. Changes that are simple and easy to interpret require no formal planning system; bright individuals who can comprehend and synthesize a few variables are adequate for the task. However, most of the complex and interrelated changes that affect modern society and its organizations are well beyond the capacity of any single individual to identify and evaluate. The day is past when a "war on poverty" can be viewed as a potential solution to the complex problems created by unemployment; educational, health, and cultural deficiencies; industrial practices; political philosophy; and a host of other elements. We have also progressed past the point where a firm that possesses only financial capital and good management resources can hope to be successful by casually investing in businesses that are unrelated to its existing technological or product-market base, as many did in the 1960s.[9] The need for a thorough and often complex strategy has now been well documented.[10]

Simple solutions will not suffice for complex problems, and simplistic mechanisms for planning only rarely produce anything but simple solutions. Thus, today's complex organizations have a need for a logical planning base that will guide them in assessing their environment, in identifying opportunities and problems, in formulating and evaluating strategy, and in implementing and controlling their strategic choices.[11] Without such a base, they may do one or a few of these things well on a fortuitous basis, but they will not do them consistently, effectively, and efficiently.

The Logical Framework
for Effective Strategic Planning

Exhibit 1-1 diagrams the logical framework for strategic planning. The dotted line encompasses the internal environment of the organization. Outside of this in the upper left are the *general environment* and the *operating environment.* (See Chapters 9 and 10 for more detailed discussions of this environmental taxonomy.) These environments represent government, the firm's industry, competitors, and other external groups and factors that are important to the outcomes of the firm's strategy. The interactions of the previously chosen strategy and these environments create consequences of prior decisions or existing situations, some of which are perceived to be symptomatic of problems. These symptoms are perceived differently by various individuals and groups.

To bring these situations, consequences, and problem symptoms into focus, the organization's strategic planning system should involve the following three categories of formal assessments:

1. Environmental opportunities and risks
2. Strategic issues
3. Organizational strengths and weaknesses

(We shall deal with these assessments in greater detail in several later chapters. Here they are dealt with only in an introductory fashion.)

Environmental Opportunities and Risks

Environmental opportunities and risks represent the organization's perceptions of the specific major environmental elements that will affect the organization's ability to achieve its goals. One such opportunity might be a new technological development that would provide the basis for a new product or would significantly affect demand for an existing one.

Strategic Issues

Strategic issues arise from general external conditions or pressures that may have similar effects on multiple aspects of a firm's operations. For instance, inflation, the energy situation, and governmental tax policy are often identified as strategic issues by business firms.

Organizational Strengths and Weaknesses

Organizational strengths and weaknesses are those characteristics of the organization that should form the foundation for its future strategy (strengths) and that should be avoided as the underpinnings of strategy (weaknesses). Thus, a firm that has production cost advantages over competitors should develop a strategy that builds on this strength. One that suffers from continuing labor unrest should avoid a strategy that depends heavily on timely deliveries or other benefits of smooth labor relations.

8

EXHIBIT 1-1

Strategic Planning Framework

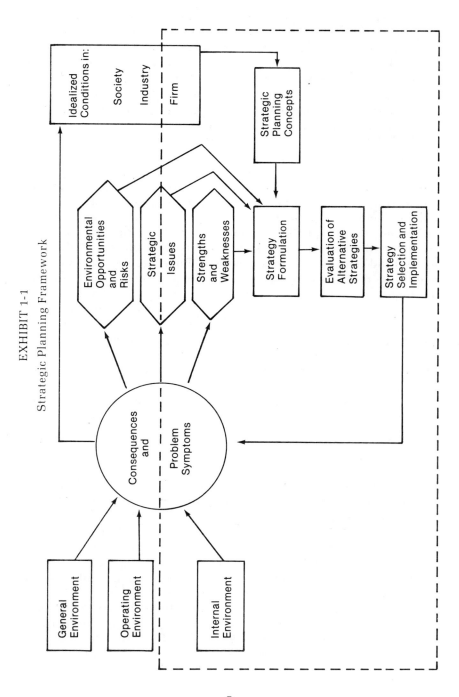

9

As Exhibit 1-1 shows, each of these assessments must be made as a part of the strategic planning process. The SPS should provide the mechanisms to permit this. Of course, all of these characteristics *may* be well known to the firm, and an SPS may not be seen as necessary for identifying them. However, the firm that holds this belief usually finds itself dealing in vague ways with nebulously defined issues, opportunities, and risks. If the elements are not clearly defined and evaluated as to their relative importance, they usually cannot be dealt with effectively. In later chapters, we deal with the operational mechanisms for making these various evaluations.

The remainder of Exhibit 1-1 shows how internal perceptions of idealized conditions in society, the industry, and the firm are influenced by reality and how they play a part, along with strategic planning concepts, in the definition and refinement of the problems and issues that form the substance of strategic decision making. (Chapter 12 contains an analysis of ways in which improved planning models and concepts can be developed.) For example, such idealized conditions might be related to the nation's economic system and how it "should" operate, the social purpose of the firm, or the role of the industry in the nation's economy. A firm's managers may think of these idealized conditions as general goals or values. However idealized they may seem to be to the uninitiated, they are very real in most firms. Some firms pursue them overtly, by refusing to engage in business practices that are inconsistent with their general goals. In other instances, the goals are pursued only implicitly in that they affect strategies through their impact on the perceptions of the managers who make the strategy choices.

Strategic Planning Concepts

The *strategic planning concepts* referred to in Exhibit 1-1 encompass broad concepts of organizational mission and objectives, as well as more specific concepts such as the way in which various business units fit into the overall portfolio of businesses in a diversified corporation. Firms that believe their mission—the "business that they are in"—to be fixed and predetermined do not treat this concept as an element of strategic planning. But missions that remain implicit often cause difficulty because they are inflexible and unchanging views of what the business is. As environmental conditions change, the mission may require change as well. A firm that has not given specific consideration to the choice of a mission is less likely to be able to appropriately adapt its mission to changing circumstances than one that has carefully thought out and developed its mission.

10

These strategic planning concepts represent standards for strategic choice against which the firm's decisions can be tested. They prompt the asking of basic questions, such as:

Have we truly decided on our mission, or have we merely accepted the mission that history has given to us?
Are our proposed actions consistent with one another?
What role does this individual part of the firm play in achieving our overall goals and purposes?

The Strategic Planning Process

In Exhibit 1-1, all of these elements feed into a process of strategic decision making which, when implemented, interacts with environmental factors to produce the next round of consequences and problems.

This planning process—which forms the vertical core of Exhibit 1-1—initially involves the evaluation of various perceptions of the environment and their synthesis into a form that is useful to the organization. For instance, each individual will have his or her own idea of the major environmental trends that will affect the business. These must be evaluated for relevance, accuracy, and validity and must then be synthesized into a form that can be used as a basis for the development of strategy. Without this evaluation and synthesis, these perceptions represent only the musings of interested individuals. When they have been so evaluated, they become a concrete basis for coherent organizational responses.

The planning process also involves the evaluation of alternative strategies, the final selection of a strategy, and its implementation. These activities may be broadly categorized as strategy formulation (an inventive or synthesizing step), strategy selection (an evaluative step), and strategy implementation (an action step).

Strategy formulation Strategy formulation involves identifying and depicting the *strategy elements* (the factors that are to be included in the firm's strategy) and specifying *alternative strategies* for consideration. This part of the process includes the consideration of the extent to which social consequences are to be considered, and what emphasis on market share and profit goals will be sought. It also involves the invention of strategies for further consideration. For example, does the company wish to consider a strategy that emphasizes the development of new markets for its products or one that emphasizes greater sales to existing customers? Does it wish to pursue product innovations or to be an imitator of innovation?

11

Strategy evaluation and selection   Once alternative strategies have been defined, the evaluation and selection part of the process begins. This involves applying criteria based on the objectives (profit, market penetration, geographic expansion) to the likely future consequences of each strategy. For instance, the evaluation must address such questions as "How likely is it that a proposed strategy will achieve desired levels of market share and profit?" Based on these assessments, a best strategy can be selected from the available alternatives.

Strategy implementation   The implementation of a chosen strategy may appear to be an obvious consequence of its choice. However, in complex organizations, the making of a choice, even by a high-level official, does not ensure that it will be carried out. Bureaucracies have their own inertia, and there are always the possibilities of communications failures, misunderstandings, or overt refusals to execute directions. Therefore, a carefully conceived implementation strategy is an essential part of the overall planning process.

Using the SPS Framework

The logical framework for strategic planning that is outlined in Exhibit 1-1 can be adapted to the needs and skills of many types of organizations. Some organizations may need a rigorous and systematic process to ensure that the various planning activities are performed well or to ensure the consideration of a wider variety of strategic alternatives than has been previously employed. Other organizations may wish to adapt the basic logical model to allow for the special creative capabilities and talents of individuals who will play a role in developing strategy.

Resources that are allocated to implement a strategic planning system should meet the same tests of effectiveness and efficiency as those that are allocated elsewhere. Thus, this book presents a flexible SPS framework that will permit elaboration and refined analyses where they are deemed to be necessary. In situations where less detailed analysis is required, the SPS is sufficiently flexible to represent only a broad guide to planning.

For example, a firm that is seeking to maintain its position through the low-cost manufacture of a mature product must have a sophisticated system for cost control to achieve price advantages in raw material purchases and state-of-the-art process technology. Such a firm might safely devote relatively modest resources to the monitor-

12

ing of new product patents, except at those points when major capital expansion is to take place.

Standing in marked contrast to the low-cost producer is the technological innovator within the industry. This firm's strategic planning system must encompass a thorough monitoring mechanism for new technology and evolving market demands. Specialized manufacturing processes may be antithetical to the firm's strategic requirements, and raw material price fluctuations may be insignificant in comparison to the firm's total value-added.

In short, a firm's strategic posture within an industry should influence the proportional distribution of resources to the elements of an SPS in a manner similar to that in which such strategic postures influence other strategic resource allocations.

Although a primary focus of this book is on the logical, analytical, and normative aspects of strategic planning, one can disregard the personal and behavioral aspects only at great risk. Strategic choices in most organizations are made by people who did not reach their positions of power through diffidence or timidity. As well, interorganizational competition and intraorganizational rivalry can often become so personal that many of the rational-analytical concepts we propose may be disregarded "in the heat of battle." Nonetheless, an executive's desire to vent some emotional response should at least be tempered by an awareness of the best available assessments of the long-term consequences to his or her organization.

The concept of strategic planning that we shall pursue is one that is consciously designed to guide the *purposive* activities of an organization. As such, the concept does not attempt to capture the full scope of executive or managerial routine or activity, or to prescribe exactly how much effort should be devoted to the planning process. Some firms will find it necessary to be involved in planning on a more or less continuous basis. Some will find that an annual planning cycle nicely prescribes the varying levels of involvement in planning throughout the year. Others will find that the existence of an annual cycle does not mean that every planning activity must be conducted each and every year.

A primary value of this logical model of planning is that it is adaptable in various ways in both directions—toward greater or lesser systematization, rationality, and logic. Thus, despite our focus on the logical basis for planning, the model presented here is not a purist's version of planning. Rather, it is one that combines logic with the wisdom which can be obtained only through practice. In effect, *it is a standard against which one's planning approach can be assessed.* And, as a standard, it can be adapted to suit the special needs and abilities of many decidedly nonstandard organizations.

13

Chapter Summary and
Overview of the Book

This chapter deals with the need for formal plans and strategy and for a strategic planning system framework that can be used to produce them. Although all firms do not need the highest degree of sophistication and formalism in their planning, they do require a model from which they can make adaptations to suit their unique needs. The framework outlined in Exhibit 1-1 is such a model.

The remainder of the book serves to elaborate on the model of Exhibit 1-1, to present variations in it that may be useful to various firms, and to indicate how various firms may wish to apply the model in different ways.

Chapter 2 elaborates the framework in terms of its differential applicability to integrated and diversified firms.

Chapters 3–8 take one important element of the framework, internal strategic analysis, and show how such an analysis can be performed in various elements of a business unit such as marketing, finance, and R&D.

Chapters 9 and 10 deal with another element of the framework, strategic environmental analysis, in terms of its practical application.

Chapter 11 departs from the single-business-unit focus of Chapters 3–10 to deal with the additional complexities that must be dealt with in diversified firms.

Chapter 12 then deals with the organizational and structural processes that are so important to the successful fulfillment of all of the approaches and techniques discussed in the book.

Notes

1. See "American Home Products: Can William Laporte Keep Those Profits Growing?" *Business Week*, October 20, 1980, pp. 80–91.

2. "Crown Cork and Seal and Metal Container Industry," Intercollegiate Case Clearing House #6-373-077.

3. "Design & Manufacturing Corporation," in C. R. Christensen et al., *Business Policy: Text and Cases*, 4th ed. (Homewood, Illinois: R. D. Irwin, 1978), pp. 416–424.

4. For a more detailed description, see Bernard Wysocki, Jr., "Sears Facing an Array of Nagging Problems," *Wall Street Journal*, December 27, 1978, p. 1; and Carol J. Loomis, "The Leaning Tower of Sears," *Fortune*, July 2, 1979, pp. 78–85.

5. T. Levitt, "Marketing Myopia," *Harvard Business Review*, July-August, 1960, pp. 45–56. (Republished by *HBR* in September-October, 1975.)

6. T. Levitt, "Dinosaurs Among the Bears and Bulls," *Harvard Business Review*, January-February, 1975, pp. 41–53; and R. Rumelt, *Strategy, Structure and Economic Performance of the Fortune 500* (Boston, Mass.: Harvard Business School, Division of Research, 1974).

Kenneth R. Graham and Max D. Richards, "Relative Performance Deterioration, Management and Strategic Change in Rail-based Holding Companies," *Academy of Management Proceedings 1979*, pp. 108–112.

D. E. Schendel and G. R. Patton, "Corporate Stagnation and Turnaround," *Journal of Economics & Business*, Vol. 28, No. 3, Spring-Summer, 1976, pp. 236–241.

7. Peter J. Schuyten, "Chrysler Goes for Broke," *Fortune*, June 19, 1978, pp. 54–56, 58.

8. H. E. Wrapp, "Good Managers Don't Make Policy Decisions," *Harvard Business Review*, September-October, 1967, pp. 91–99.

9. See, for instance, "You Can Be Sure If It's Industrial-Westinghouse," *Iron Age*, March 3, 1975, pp. 20–25.

10. See M. S. Salter and W. A. Weinhold, *Diversification Through Acquisition: Strategies for Creating Economic Value* (New York: The Free Press, 1979).

11. This process of systematically relating an organization to its external environment for purposes of survival and growth has been referred to by Professor Charles Summer as *comprehensive alignment*. Charles E. Summer, "Comprehensive Alignment: Strategy and Policy Formulation," in *Strategic Behavior in Business and Government* (Boston: Little, Brown & Company, 1980), chapter 5.

CHAPTER 2

Strategic Planning in Integrated and Diversified Firms

THIS CHAPTER will extend the strategic planning framework that was introduced in Chapter 1 by demonstrating its application in both *integrated* (single business) and *diversified* (multibusiness) firms. At an abstract level, it is possible to treat strategy making as a similar task in all firms, but there is a great deal of evidence that the differences are great enough to warrant separate treatment. Therefore, the basic framework of Chapter 1 will be adapted in two general directions— one applying to integrated firms and the other to diversified firms.

Integrated firms range in size from small family-owned retail outlets to large integrated steel companies, but they have the common characteristic of being involved in a relatively narrow range of customer, product, and technological activities. Hence, it is feasible to expect that a single experienced executive will be able to comprehend the interdependencies among the various activities. To some degree, this means that formal organizational planning processes reinforce the planning that is routinely done by individual executives in such firms. However, as integrated firms grow large and complex, they need an overall planning process to organize the planning activities that may be carried on by their various departments and subunits.

Diversified firms, on the other hand, operate in a variety of environments, with different sets of customers and competitors and often with different process technologies. Many operate as conglomerates which own or control numerous other companies, each identified with a particular product line and markets. For instance, ITT owns and operates such diverse businesses as the Sheraton Corporation (hotels), Continental Baking Company, Standard Telephones & Cables, Ltd., and Hartford Fire Insurance Company.

16

Diversified firms must use strategic concepts of *portfolio balance* and *risk management* in a much more sophisticated manner than is necessary in an integrated organization. (*Portfolio* is a term borrowed from the area of financial management, where it describes a collection of investments, such as bonds and common stocks, each of which has different characteristics in terms of return, growth potential, risk, etc. Here it is applied to a collection of business units that have different sets of such characteristics.) This is because their various businesses face different environments, with different growth patterns, future prospects, and business cycles. Thus, the balancing of these diverse businesses in terms of profitability and risk becomes of paramount importance.

Such firms have great intrinsic need for formal planning processes, since it is not reasonable to expect any individual or group to have an intuitive understanding of all the possible interrelationships of the various businesses, functions, types of technology, and so forth.

In one sense, of course, a diversified firm is simply a collection of single product firms or businesses. This means that it must both perform effective planning at the business level and integrate this planning with corporate-level planning activities. However, a diversified firm has the potential to be much more than the sum of its parts. The idea of *synergy* is central to the rationale for the existence of such enterprises. Synergy may exist in a variety of corporate dimensions, such as markets, costs, technology, and management. If it can be created and used to advantage, a diversified firm may prosper to a degree that is beyond the cumulative potential of its constituent parts.

The Nature of Strategy in Integrated and Diversified Firms

Exhibit 2-1 shows the strategy relationships in integrated and diversified firms in terms of corporate, business, and functional levels of planning activity.

The integrated firm synthesizes functional activities, such as those involving marketing and production, into a single integrated strategy. For single market firms, such corporate-level activities as securing financing, designing organizational relationships, and developing managers are tied directly to the production and selling functions. Thus, corporate-level and business-level planning is much the same in such firms.

In the diversified firm, there is a distinct separation between corporate-level planning functions and those on the business level, as

17

EXHIBIT 2-1

Strategy Levels in Two Classes of Firms

	Class of firm	
Levels of planning	Integrated or single market firm	Diversified or multiple market firm
Corporate Level	Single Integrated Strategy	Portfolio and Organizational Strategy
Business Level	↑ ↑ ↑ *synthesize*	Various Business-unit or Industry-level Strategies ↑ ↑ ↑ *synthesize*
Functional Level	Functional Operations	Functional Operations

shown in Exhibit 2-1. The relationship of the individual business headquarters to the functional-level departments in a diversified firm is similar to that in an integrated firm. However, planning on the corporate level involves the determination of how the business unit can compete most effectively with the expected level of corporate financial support. At the corporate level, consideration is primarily devoted to portfolio balance, overall growth objectives, and the allocation of funds and goals to the various individual businesses.

Strategic Organizational Characteristics of Integrated and Diversified Firms

There are various clear organizational differences between integrated and diversified firms. These differences have strategic implications that explain the need for two different adaptations of the basic planning framework.

The salient differences are summarized in Exhibit 2-2 in terms of *structural* and *task* dimensions of the two varieties of organization. Structural characteristics are assessed in the top portion of the exhibit, while the task dimensions are treated in the lower portion.

Structural Differences between Integrated and Diversified Firms

The basic structures of integrated and diversified firms create their own strategic demands, which must be accounted for in the process

18

of strategic planning and management. These are presented in the top portion of Exhibit 2-2 in terms of the formal organization, time frames, evaluation criteria, and incentive systems.

The formal organization The integrated firm has a formal organization that consists of specialized functional departments that are highly dependent on one another for efficient conversion processes. In diversified firms, the primary organizational subunits are divisions

EXHIBIT 2-2

Strategic Organizational Differences
between Integrated and Diversified
Firms

Organizational dimensions	Class of firm	
	Integrated	Diversified
Structural Characteristics		
Formal organization	Departments related by *function*	Multifunctional divisions to serve separate markets
Time frames	Related to production and demand cycles for the primary product	Related to product life cycles and portfolio positions of divisions
Criteria for evaluating subunits	Technical and/or cost standards for each function	Investment efficiency over time
Incentive system for subunits	Related to technical performance and length of service	Variable rewards linked to economic performance of the subunit
Tasks		
Nature of strategic choice	Balance *functional departments* toward a single market	Balance a portfolio of *businesses* among multiple markets
Transactions among subunits	Through specialized departments to a single market	From individual strategic business units to separate markets
Focus of innovation	Search for product or process improvements	Search for new product-market concepts as well as improvements

Source: Material in this illustration is adapted from the stages of organizational development model presented by Bruce R. Scott in "The New Industrial State: Old Myths and New Realities," *Harvard Business Review*, March-April, 1973, pp. 133–148; and the analyses of Jay R. Galbraith and Daniel A. Nathanson in "The Role of Organizational Structure & Process in Strategy Implementation," *Strategic Management* (Boston: Little, Brown and Company, 1979), pp. 249–283.

19

that are responsible for both their own sources of materials and their own customers. As a result, the primary corporate-level concerns in most diversified firms are with cash flow patterns that will facilitate the execution of desired activities and with the development of effective divisional managers. In such firms, corporate-level coordination primarily requires the management of cash flows among divisions to minimize the costs of using external financing sources.[1]

Time frames A second structural characteristic that has different strategic implications for integrated and diversified firms is the nature of the time frames that must be considered in making strategic choices. Production and demand cycles in one specific industry are of primary concern in the integrated firm, because they dictate the allocation of investment between working capital and fixed investment and influence the rate of capacity changes within that industry sector. The diversified firm, in contrast, must balance over time the sometimes interdependent economic demands of numerous strategic business units (SBUs) that operate in different industry sectors.

This situation provides diversified firms with opportunities that are not tied to particular production and demand cycles. These opportunities may be reflected in changes in portfolio composition, industry position, growth or contraction, or interactions with capital markets and suppliers. All of these are major strategic moves that can be more freely made in the diversified environment because of the balance that may be provided by the diversity.

Evaluation criteria In integrated firms, the evaluation of performance focuses on technical or cost-based standards at the subunit level. For instance, the production department may be assessed in terms of its efficiency in using resources per unit of output. Thus, wasted materials and machine idle time become measures of concern. The marketing department may be assessed in terms of success in achieving sales quotas or reducing budgeted expenses. All of these are useful, but limited, measures of the department's real contribution to what the firm is trying to achieve. This narrow focus is necessary because the actual overall economic contribution is difficult to measure. Thus, in integrated firms the performance of subunits is assessed in terms of input or process measures rather than output measures such as profit contribution. Overall performance is, of course, assessed in output terms, but the contribution of individual subunits to the firms' total output may, in fact, never be assessed.

The diversified firm with a divisional structure is not faced with the same problem of measurement. It is possible to fairly accurately

20

assess the economic contributions of individual SBUs. However, there is evidence that many divisionalized firms have not yet refined their internal measurement systems to the satisfaction of divisional managers.[2]

Incentive systems The incentive systems for subunit managers in integrated firms are closely related to their specialized competence and tenure with the firm. Because there is seldom a good way to relate economic results to the individual performance of such managers, it is not possible to use variable compensation arrangements geared to return on investment (ROI) or other profitability measures. Diversified firms have the advantage of economic separability among subunits, which permits them to implement bonus payments or other variable incentives in direct relationship to ROI or other appropriate performance measures.

Task Differences between Integrated and Diversified Firms

Several task differences between integrated and diversified firms have important strategic implications. These are shown in the lower portion of Exhibit 2-2 as strategic choice, transactions among subunits, and the focus of innovation.

The nature of strategic choice Among the major strategic tasks of the management in both classes of firms is the efficient balancing of cash inflows and the uses to which resources are put. The major internally oriented strategic choice problem in integrated firms is one of balancing the investment pattern among the functional departments over time in a manner that supports the desired product-market positioning. This must be done without unnecessarily adding inefficient increments of capacity or activity. For example, many marketing activities can be increased efficiently in very small increments, but a new unit of refining capacity or a meaningful R&D project may be feasible only on a large scale. The failure to synchronize and balance such commitments can lead to waste in the form of premature investment or inefficient additions.

The comparable corporate-level strategic choice in the diversified firm involves the balancing of cash flows, cyclicality, and growth or decline patterns for various businesses within the corporation over time. The responsibility for efficient resource allocation among the functional areas is then delegated to the various business unit managers to execute in accordance with the market position goal that each business pursues.

Transactions among subunits A second major task that distinguishes the two varieties of firms involves the product or service transactions among subunits. In integrated firms, there is a requirement for sequential coordination from engineering through manufacturing to marketing and then to the customer. As a result, a high level of dependence must exist among the subunits if efficiency is to be obtained. Thus, interdepartmental cooperation must be nurtured.

The diversified firm, on the other hand, often has very limited transactions among the operating divisions, so there may be relatively little need to foster cooperation. In fact, competition among business units for the available investment funds may create interdivisional conflict and even hostility. The closest organizational linkages, therefore, often extend vertically from the corporate office to the division and then to the market it serves.

The focus of innovation Another important task that influences the organizational relationships and the strategic planning approaches in the two classes of firms involves the search for innovation. The integrated firm must guide its R&D investments in a narrow search for incremental improvements in product design or process technology so that its market position can be protected and existing production facilities do not become prematurely obsolete.

Although R&D activities may be organized in a variety of ways in diversified firms, the general performance objectives include both totally new product-market opportunities and improvements in existing products and manufacturing processes. For many such firms, the process of managing innovation is more one of focusing resources on a potentially fruitful problem than it is of ensuring that the activities have immediate relevance to the present operations of the firm.

Strategic Implications of the Structural and Task Differences

In the many ways outlined in Exhibit 2-2, the differences in structural and task dimensions between integrated and diversified firms imply quite different demands for effective strategic management.

The strategic managers of the integrated firm are more intimately involved in the identification of discrepancies or performance gaps among the functional activities of the firm than are their counterparts in the diversified firm.[3] The organizational system that they must strategically manage is best characterized in terms of flows of materials, information, and other resources among functional entities. In structural terms, their emphasis must lie in the stimulation of cooperation and coordination toward the efficient attainment of a focused product-market position.

In the diversified firm, strategic management primarily involves the economic coordination of multiple product-market positions and the guidance of "managed rivalry" among division executives, all of whom have strategic options in their own sectors and all of whom may be providing significantly different economic consequences for the corporation's business portfolio. Strategic management in this sort of system largely involves consideration of balance, the allocation of differential financial support, and the design of appropriate incentive and control systems.

Strategic Planning in the Integrated Firm

The planning framework outlined in Chapter 1 may be readily adapted to suit the unique strategy characteristics of the integrated single market firm. Exhibit 2-3 shows such an adaptation in detail.

At the top of the diagram is an assessment of the general environment. This feeds into an assessment of the operating environment on the right of the diagram. At the left is an assessment of the internal environment. These three assessments represent a well-accepted taxonomy.[4]

Internal Environment—The elements that are within the firm's official jurisdiction

Operating Environment—The set of suppliers, customers, and interest groups with which the firm deals directly

General Environment—The national and global context of social, political, regulatory, economic, and technological conditions

This is a useful way of thinking about the firm's environment because the three levels are distinguishable in terms of the degree of control and influence that the organization can exert and the information that is typically available to it. In general, the degree of control and the availability of information are greatest in the internal environment and least in the general environment. However, it is one of the purposes of planning to increase, if possible, the degree of influence that may be exerted on the environment and to obtain better information than what is readily available. This proactive view of planning, therefore, focuses on the operating and general environmental levels, where the amount of natural control and information is most limited.

23

EXHIBIT 2-3

Strategic Planning Process
in a Single Market Firm

```
                    ┌─────────────────────────┐
                    │   General Environment    │
                    │ ------------------------ │
                    │ Societal expectations    │
                    │ Capital markets          │
                    │ Governmental incentives  │
                    │   and constraints        │
                    │ Etc.                     │
                    └─────────────────────────┘

┌──────────────────────────┐      ┌──────────────────────────┐
│   Internal Environment    │      │  Operating Environment    │
│ ------------------------- │      │ ------------------------- │
│ Financial resources       │      │ Competitors               │
│ Technology                │      │   size, skills, etc.      │
│ Market position           │      │ Suppliers                 │
│ Human skills              │      │ Customers                 │
│ Etc.                      │      │ Etc.                      │
└──────────────────────────┘      └──────────────────────────┘

                    ╭─────────────────╮
                    │   Compare and   │
                    │    Analyze      │
                    │  Relationships  │
                    ╰─────────────────╯

┌──────────────────────────┐      ┌──────────────────────────┐
│ Aspirations and           │      │ Market Opportunities and  │
│ Perceived Relative        │      │ Competitive Threats       │
│ Competencies              │      │                           │
└──────────────────────────┘      └──────────────────────────┘

              ┌──────────────────────────┐
              │  Strategic Alternatives   │
              └──────────────────────────┘

              ┌──────────────────────────┐
              │ Choice of                 │
              │ Market Segments and       │
              │ Competitive Methods       │
              └──────────────────────────┘

        ┌──────────────────────────────────┐
        │ Implementation of Processes       │
        │ and Realignment of Resources      │
        └──────────────────────────────────┘

              ┌──────────────────────────┐
              │  Competitive              │
              │  Interaction              │
              └──────────────────────────┘

┌────────────┐  ┌──────────────────┐  ┌──────────────────┐
│ Reallocate │  │ Consequences     │  │ Stimulate        │
│ Resources  │  │ of Performance   │  │ Adaptation       │
└────────────┘  └──────────────────┘  └──────────────────┘
```

24

Internal Strategic Assessment

The internal strategic assessment at the left of Exhibit 2-3 involves the evaluation of the firm's existing market position and the supporting technical, financial, and human resources. It should yield important conclusions about the organization's current position and capabilities. The assessment of capabilities and strengths that can be the basis of future strategy is particularly important.

The other major element of the assessment of the current position has to do with the relative strengths of the firm when compared with those of competitors and resource suppliers within the operating segment of the environment. Chapters 3–8 deal with the details of internal strategic analyses in the various functional areas of a business.

External Strategic Assessment

The strategic assessment of the operating and general environments is perhaps best described through an elaboration of the internal-operating-general taxonomy. This is shown in Exhibit 2-4, where the operating environment is divided into such elements as suppliers and employee unions. The general environment contains such elements as regulatory agencies, the social environment, and the technological environment. The specification of these subsystems will vary for different organizations and according to particular purposes within a single organization. In one case, for instance, it may be necessary for an organization to distinguish individual regulatory agencies. For other purposes, it may be adequate to group all such agencies together into a single homogeneous group.

Although the macro and micro environmental models appear to be simple enough, there are a number of difficulties that may arise when one tries to fit them to a particular situation.

One such difficulty is created when a subsystem element overlaps the operating and general environments. For example, the Federal Communications Commission (FCC) can exert a general corporate-level constraint by limiting the number of AM or FM radio stations owned by a single corporation. It can, however, also influence the operating environment at the business unit level, as in the case of Texas Instruments' efforts to secure a waiver of certain FCC technical requirements pertaining to the linkage of home computers to television monitors.[5] The significance of a single environmental variable in this example is dramatic—a waiver would permit a 50 percent reduction in retail prices early in the product life cycle. Although this

EXHIBIT 2-4

Environmental Subsystems:
Three Levels of Analysis

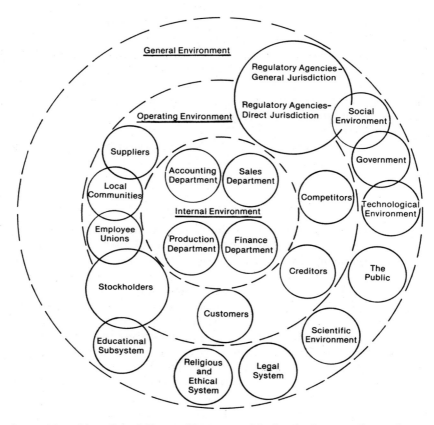

Source: Adapted from Philip S. Thomas, "Environmental Analysis for Corporate Planning," *Business Horizons,* October, 1974, p. 28. Copyright © 1974 by Business Horizons.

example of Texas Instruments' "home computer problem" focuses on the regulatory issue, it should be noted that the basis for the waiver request is a technical problem of potential interference with radio or TV broadcasting. Hence, there is a second level of interaction among the seemingly separate technical and regulatory subsystems.

The arena of merger regulation provides another example of the way in which a given environmental shift or trend can be viewed as an operating subsystem by one part of a corporation and as a general subsystem by another.[6] Such diverse firms as Litton Industries, Reliance Electric (now a division of Exxon), and Xerox have, through acquisitions, extended their technical and marketing capacities within an industry; business-level strategies were intimately linked to the firms' capacity to avoid the time-consuming efforts required for internal development. Regulatory shifts might make small acquisitions easier or related acquisitions for large companies almost impossible—the industry-level consequences would obviously be dramatically different. Corporations that have built their corporate strategies around the profit potential from acquisition and divestiture activity, such as Fuqua Industries, could find a very hostile general environment as a result of restrictive merger regulation.[7]

Another level of interdependency that is demonstrated in Exhibit 2-4 is one that often exists among subsystems. For example, the local community may comprise many people who are employees and others who are suppliers. In addition, the stockholders may include both the employees' pension fund and the endowment trusts of several universities from the educational subsystem. The process of neatly separating people who play multiple roles into a single subsystem can be quite misleading, so the level of interdependency among some of the important subsystems should receive explicit attention. In the opinion of some researchers, the study of these environmental subsystem interactions may be one of the most critical aspects of strategic planning in the years ahead.

The fact that not all elements of the environment are alike adds to the complexity of developing a structure to describe that environment. Some elements are more predictable than others; some are constantly changing, while others change only slowly. The conducting of external environmental strategic analyses will be treated in detail in Chapters 9 and 10, using the internal and external strategic assessments.

Returning to the basic SPS framework of Exhibit 2-3, we see that after the assessments of the internal and external environments are made, a comparative analysis takes place, as shown in the circle in the center of the diagram.

The perceived position of the firm within the identified environment influences the executives' level of aspiration and their subsequent search for alternatives. These goals are then combined with an assessment of the technological, regulatory, and other changes that are altering the strategic options within the industry. It is at this point that the ability to forecast shifting customer interests and levels of competitive aggressiveness shows that some strategic alternatives should be evaluated immediately while others should be deferred until a later time. From among the available strategies that merit current evaluation, the executives should choose one that has a reasonable probability of fulfilling their objectives. These strategic alternatives are shown just below the center of Exhibit 2-3 as the next sequential phase of the process.

This approach to the generation of strategic alternatives is a very pragmatic one. It is an application of bounded rationality—the antithesis of academic approaches to problem solving, which presume that all alternatives must be specified and evaluated.[8]

The alternatives specified in this process are a narrow selection from the domain of all that are available. They are those that:

Emphasize the firm's strengths and deemphasize its weaknesses;
Emphasize a comparative advantage that the firm may possess over its competitors;
Are consistent with the values and aspirations of the owners and executives;
Are in concert with environmental trends and the opportunities they will create.

The specific choices of which market segment to pursue and which methods of competition to employ—the next level of the strategic process in Exhibit 2-3—often serve to spark conflict, because it is at this point that abstract notions of excellence or service must be considered in real terms such as product design, distribution channels, or the quality of a work force.

This is also the time at which the amount of change that is really feasible may become an issue, since the economic independence of a firm will largely determine the rate at which it can realistically depart from a previously existing strategy. For instance, publicly held firms may find that some attractive long-term options are so costly in the short term that executives' jobs or corporate autonomy would be jeopardized by pursuing them.

At the next level of the process shown in Exhibit 2-3, the implementation of organizational processes and the realignment of resources to achieve internal consistency or complementary relationships among the various functions (such as marketing and technology) becomes the paramount concern.

The alignment of resources for the implementation of strategy involves the synchronization of effort in each of the functional areas, so that activities will complement or reinforce one another rather than work at cross purposes. For example, a strategy conceived to offer a low-priced consumer product to the mass market might emphasize quantity purchases of raw materials, long production runs of standardized items, and distribution through chains of discount stores or similar outlets. A production manager who sought to customize the products or produce them in small batches "as the orders arrived" would be inadvertently undermining the strategy based on low costs.

As shown at the bottom of Exhibit 2-3, when activities in each of the functional areas are shifted toward a chosen product-market objective, competitors and customers will begin to sense the evolving changes and thus seek to modify their behavior accordingly. The assessment and interpretation of the consequences of an evolving strategy is usually difficult, particularly during the important early stages, because it is frequently unclear which changes can be attributed directly to strategic actions and which are the result of competitors' inaction or other outside factors. The interpretations attached to the apparent results of strategic actions by both the initiating firm and others within the industry are extremely important, however, because they will influence the next sequence of adaptive behavior. Needless to say, the consequences will be quite different if an arch-rival views a particular action as a "careless mistake" rather than as a "daring and threatening innovation." As a result, substantive moves are often accompanied by various forms of signaling in order to reduce the speed or strength of countermoves being considered by competitors.

The overall sequence of scanning, analysis, choice, and action of Exhibit 2-3 is repeated continuously in large, formally organized single market firms and somewhat more sporadically in smaller firms, particularly those that exist in rather tranquil operating environments. In either case, the single market focus that is common to this class of firm means that there is a rather stable commitment to a particular market segment and that the strategic dimensions of that commitment can be understood and synthesized by a single individual.

Strategic Planning in Multiple Market or Diversified Firms

Firms that have divided their corporate resources among several substantially different markets require a more sophisticated planning process entailing activities that extend beyond the domain of those found in the single product firm.

It has been estimated that among the 500 largest firms in the nation the proportion that would be categorized as single business has declined from about 35 percent in 1949 to about 6 percent in 1969, while the proportion of conglomerates has increased from less than 3 percent to 19 percent. Growth in the number of multibusiness firms that have related businesses (those sharing markets, technology, or other characteristics) has been pronounced as well during this period.[9] Thus, not only is planning more complex in such firms, but since they are becoming more pervasive, this more complex variety of planning is coming to be of greater overall significance for knowledgeable managers.

Exhibit 2-5 shows how the planning framework of Chapter 1 can be adapted to meet the special needs of the diversified firm. It shows a distinct separation between the corporate-level functions of financing, organizational structuring, and portfolio balancing and those at the business or SBU level.

As we did in the single market firm discussion, we shall address the components of the exhibit with a focus on strategic change, even though the planning process may finally show that no change in strategy is required.

In the diversified firm, this emphasis on change is particularly appropriate because the divisional or business unit form of structure provides greater flexibility for entering and leaving markets. There is great opportunity for corporate-level planners to explore objectives and aspirations without the immediate, and often overwhelming, concern for existing product-market relationships that is characteristic of most single market firms.

Exhibit 2-5 shows that corporate executives in diversified firms may consider their preferences among broad product-market categories, capital structure alternatives, and certain organizational relationships before choosing specific product-market positions. This separation of corporate-level strategic decisions from those at the divisional or SBU level provides an opportunity for a level of personal detachment from specific product-market positions that is difficult to achieve in single market firms. In exchange for this advantage, however, executives must cope with the additional complexities of having to analyze and choose combinations of subunit strategies that will provide synergy and complementary economic benefits.

The internal environment assessment at the left of Exhibit 2-5 shows that the process of assessing the strategic competencies of individual subunits in relationship to operating environmental conditions is similar in the multimarket firm to that previously discussed for the single product firm. However, because of the greater corporate resource base in relationship to a given SBU's position, the opportunity exists for the multimarket firm to make significant changes more quickly in a given industry than would typically be possible for a single market firm. In other words, the diversified firm is in a better position to seriously consider a broader array of strategic alternatives within each industry than is the typical single market firm. The desir-

30

EXHIBIT 2-5

Corporate-level Strategic Planning Process
in a Multiple Market Firm

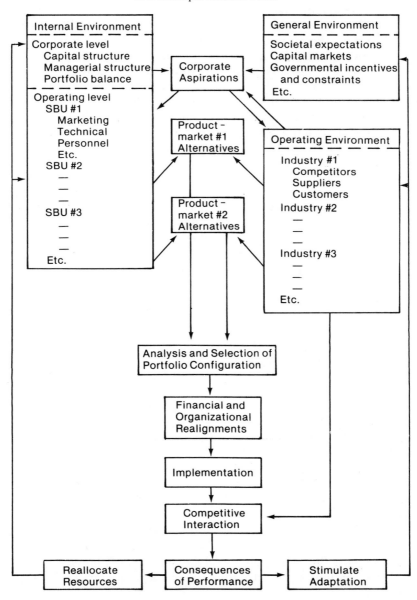

ability of certain options within each industry is constrained, however, by decisions that the corporate executives may need to make regarding other SBUs in the corporation's business portfolio.

This assessment, taken together with those of the general environment and the several operating environments, as shown at the right of Exhibit 2-5, affects corporate aspirations and the evaluation of specific product-market alternatives (both those now being pursued by the various business units and those new ones that are being considered).

Therefore, after having stimulated the various division managers to explore a small set of distinctly different strategies, the corporate executives are in a position to choose a limited number of significant changes in SBU objectives. Limitations on managerial time and stockholders' expectations typically prohibit the making of more than a few major changes each year, so the majority of SBUs will be fine tuning their ongoing strategies in response to competitors' adaptations from the prior year. The executives' interpretations of the collective market responses will stimulate questions regarding needed revisions at the corporate level in financial structure, organizational relationships, new SBUs, and so forth.

These implemented strategies and realignments, as evaluated by the external environments, affect the next round of strategic choices through feedback loops shown at the bottom of Exhibit 2-5.

The Administrative Planning Cycle in the Diversified Firm

The planning processes described in Exhibit 2-3 and Exhibit 2-5 are *substantive planning processes* in the sense that they describe the substance of *what* is to be done at each step. Associated with these substantive processes are *administrative planning cycles* that prescribe *how* the various steps are to be performed and how they relate to the various levels of the organization. In the integrated firm, the substantive planning process of Exhibit 2-3 is nearly identical with the administrative planning process. However, in a diversified firm the substantive process and the administrative process are more complex.

Since corporate-level planners typically could not possibly perform assessments of each and every business unit and operating environment, these business-level inputs to the planning process must, in fact, initially be provided to the corporate level by business unit executives and planners. Exhibit 2-6 shows how this administrative planning process works in diversified firms at the corporate, business, and functional levels.

32

EXHIBIT 2-6

Administrative Planning Process
in Diversified Firms

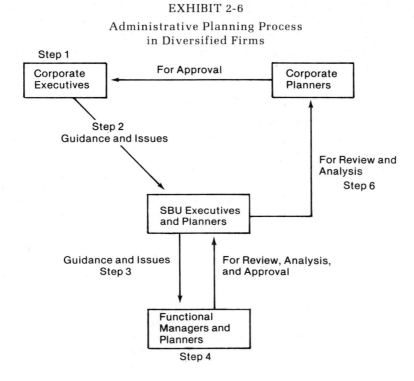

The administrative planning process is an iterative feedback process that begins when corporate-level executives and planners have performed their preliminary analysis of the internal, general, and operating environments and have begun to develop their aspirations (step 1 on the diagram). These preliminary analyses are translated into guidelines and definitions of issues for use in the formulation of preliminary SBU plans (step 2).

A similar process of providing guidance and defining issues operates between the business unit and functional levels (step 3). Plans are tentatively formulated (step 4) and submitted upward for review, analysis, and approval (steps 5 and 6).

The whole cycle normally operates several times in partial form. For instance, sometimes only a partial plan will be requested for the first cycle. Often, a comprehensive financial plan will be deferred to a later cycle to ensure that strategic considerations, rather than financial ones, are paramount in the early cycles.

In a large diversified firm, there may be more organizational levels than those shown in Exhibit 2-6. These may be called companies, sectors, or groups. When such additional hierarchical levels exist, the administrative planning process generally conducted is a variation of that shown in which several levels are stacked atop one another. In other words, an SBU's plans might be reviewed at the group level and sent back for revision before the group level submits its plans to the corporate level.

Summary

This chapter shows how the basic SPS framework of Chapter 1 can be adapted in two general directions to meet the needs of integrated and diversified firms.

These two varieties of firms require strategies that are of a fundamentally different nature because of structural differences and task differences between the two kinds of firms. The structural differences that are considered are the formal organization, time frames, criteria for subunit evaluation, and incentive systems for subunits. The task differences are the nature of the strategic choices, transactions among subunits, and the focus of innovation. Each of these differences has important implications for the determination of the strategy most appropriate for the type of firm. These differences also imply that different adaptations of the strategic planning framework will be required to generate the different strategies.

The planning process should theoretically operate on a continuous basis in both types of firms. However, many firms find it desirable to hold their chosen strategies relatively constant over some period of time and to perform major elements of the planning process on a regular annual cycle. This seems to be a satisfactory mode, so long as it does not lead to an inability to reevaluate strategy when there is evidence that the current strategy is not effective.

It is easiest to describe these processes in terms of the perception of the need for changes in strategic posture and the implementation of those changes, because the value of the approach can be best demonstrated in that way. Clearly this does not imply that strategies should be constantly shifting. Even if a rigorous scanning of the evolving environment shows that no strategy alterations are necessary, the planning process has value in assuring management that the effective strategy is one that has been selected rather than one imposed by historical precedent.

Notes

1. For further insights into the implications of formal structure, see S. Lee Jerrell, "Managing in a Hierarchy," *Managing*, no. 3, 1979, pp. 25–29.

2. Richard F. Vancil, *Decentralization: Managerial Ambiguity by Design* (Homewood, Illinois: Dow-Jones-Irwin, 1979), pp. 89–91.

3. Robert W. Ackerman, "Influence of Integration and Diversity on the Investment Process," *Administrative Science Quarterly*, September, 1970, pp. 341-351.

4. Philip S. Thomas, "Environmental Analysis for Corporate Planning," *Business Horizons*, October, 1974, pp. 26-38.

5. "TI Gets Set to Move into Home Computers," *Business Week*, March 19, 1979, p. 37.

6. Lawrence Rout, "Specter of Legislation Spurs Merger Activity, More Big Deals Loom," *Wall Street Journal*, February 2, 1979, p.1.

7. "Fuqua Says It Bought National Industries for a Bargain Price," *Wall Street Journal*, March 5, 1979, p. 32.

8. Herbert A. Simon, *Models of Man* (New York: John Wiley and Sons, 1957).

9. R. Rumelt, *Strategy, Structure and Economic Performance* (Boston: Division of Research, Harvard Graduate School of Business, 1974).

PART II

STRATEGIC ANALYSIS
AT THE
BUSINESS UNIT LEVEL

CHAPTER 3

Overall
Strategic Analysis

THIS CHAPTER is the first of a series of six dealing with the *internal analyses* that are elements of the planning frameworks developed in the first two chapters. These analyses may be conducted at the corporate level in an integrated firm or at the business unit level in a diversified firm. They are aimed at identifying and focusing the *comparative advantages* or *distinctive competencies* that the firm or business unit may be able to exploit.

In these chapters, we present methods and approaches for assessing and employing these advantages and competencies. In effect, the chapters provide the detailed substance for the internal assessment blocks that are shown on the left sides of Exhibit 2-3 (for the single business integrated firm) and Exhibit 2-5 (for the diversified firm). We shall generally use the *business unit* terminology, which is strictly applicable to a single unit of a diversified firm. However, all of the approaches are equally appropriate at the corporate level in the single business integrated firm.

This chapter presents some introductory ideas on internal business unit analyses as they relate to the overall strategic position of the business unit. Subsequent chapters deal with the conduct of internal analyses in specific areas of business operation.

We first deal with the notion of comparative advantage, because it should guide one's thinking in conducting all internal analyses. We next provide an approach to performing a preliminary overall competitive strategy analysis. Despite the fact that this is not internal to the firm, it is necessary if the competitive advantage concept is to be carried throughout the various internal analyses. Then, a widely used overall strategic position assessment model, called the *business screen*, is presented as a way of summing up a great amount of information in a form that is useful and easy to understand. Finally, the chapter deals with one of the obvious categories of overall strategies that a business unit will inevitably consider—forward or backward integration—as a means of further understanding how the position of the business unit may be assessed.

Identifying and Employing
Comparative Advantage and Distinctive Competence

To be effective, a strategy must be built on a foundation of comparative advantages or distinctive competencies that the firm possesses. *Comparative advantage* is a term borrowed from economics; it refers to the relative competencies, by functional area, of industry participants. The advantage may be in terms of such factors as the relative cost of raw materials, the relatively higher skill of the firm's artisans, or the unique reputation of a product line. For comparative advantages to have impact on the performance of the firm, they must be realistically assessed and used in a balanced fashion. *Distinctive competence* usually refers to a group of functional skills which, when exercised in concert, provide a competitive advantage.

Realistic Assessment of Comparative Advantage

Comparative advantages must be real if they are to have significant strategic impact. Sometimes firms rely on past competencies that have become outdated. Sometimes competencies are mere "slogans of superiority"—for example, "leader in technology" or "super service." For instance, one firm became so proud of its custom engineering skills it failed to recognize that it was being squeezed into the high risk, low margin segment of the market by competitors who were focusing on standardized products that would service the middle 80 percent of the market. Fortunately, the manufacturer acknowledged the phenomenon after careful market segmentation and product line cost analyses, and was able to reduce the scope of its product line and shift much of the special engineering expense to the few customers who could not utilize standardized products and were willing to pay the extra cost.

Implementing Comparative Advantage

The mere existence of a comparative advantage is of modest significance unless it can be implemented, sold, or otherwise exploited. For example, one firm might have the most sophisticated manufacturing process within its industry, but if such a process cannot yield products of superior quality or significantly lower cost, there might be no way in which to gain real benefits from the advantage. A microwave cooking capability may offer little value to a restaurant that offers home-cooked meals in a retirement community, but, on the other hand, it may offer substantial advantage to a fast-food restaurant in a busy airport.

Balance and Comparative Advantage

Very few business units secure competitive strength through the exercise of a single competence, such as capital structure, production efficiency, or personnel skills. The logic of strategic management dictates that one exploit a balanced combination of competitive competencies that will secure advantages that are more immediately recognizable to customers than to competitors.

Securing the desired level of balance is difficult, because perfect balance is not feasible for a firm that is shifting its strategy. On the other hand, too great an imbalance can cause the organization to experience unproductive disruptions. For instance, consider the people who run the various functional units. If those in R&D have a skill level that greatly exceeds that of the personnel in the other functional areas, they may serve only to inflate expenses or they may become disenchanted when people in marketing, production, and other areas are not able to carry through with their ideas. Thus, there is a clear need for a balance of skills if operations are to be effectively conducted.

Similarly, since all of the functional areas place demands on the financial resources of the enterprise, the treasury function must balance the cash demands for working capital from marketing against those for new equipment which may originate in the manufacturing plant or R&D laboratory.

However, changes or shifts in the strategic posture of the business require that some imbalances be created. A firm may only be able to expand a manufacturing facility in units of $10 million, while it can expand its sales force one person at a time. Another firm may undergo an opposite imbalance. For instance, a firm introducing a line of corporate aircraft may find it desirable to hire and train a national sales and service force of several hundred people so that customers will place orders for significant numbers of the new product, while the production activity may be so labor intensive and customized that production capacity can be expanded in relatively small increments.

Thus, modifications in strategic posture must encompass a tolerance for resource imbalance and the likely resulting inefficiencies during any strategic transitional phase. This means that the strategist must develop a keen awareness of the functional interdependencies and the level of balance that is consistent with the chosen strategy.

41

In seeking balance, the strategist must also keep in mind the evolving mosaic of strategies being pursued by competitors. An imbalance created for the purpose of achieving strategic change may play into the hands of competitors if it does not take their strategies into account.

The assessment of comparative advantage initially must be done on a function-by-function basis. Subsequently, issues of interdependence and balance among the functions may be addressed. The remainder of this chapter deals with approaches to making this assessment in terms of an overall competitive analysis.

The overall competitive analysis represents both a starting and an ending point for internal analyses. The conduct of such an overall analysis, itself involving all of the functional areas, will provide the insight and knowledge that is essential to the efficient conduct of the more detailed functional analyses. Areas in which data are deficient will be identified, as will areas in which judgments are necessary. Once detailed analyses in the various functional areas have been conducted, an overall competitive analysis can be prepared as a summary of that which has been accomplished.

Overall Competitive Strategy Analysis

Although most managers would agree that there is a need to know the competition, all too often firms actually rely primarily on their own perceptions of competitors rather than on more objective data.

An adaptation of the matrix in Exhibit 3-1 is a useful format in which to show the strategies of all firms in the relative position of the competitive arena, including one's own firm. It is useful in assessing the overall position one occupies in relation to competitors. It shows the competitive factors at both the corporate and the business unit levels in multimarket firms, because the corporate resources, particularly financial and managerial, in large part determine the potential future behavior of the subunits. This mode of analysis presumes an active corporate-level management role and discounts the adage, popular with many, that "corporations don't have competition; only business units do."

Much of the comparative analysis of Exhibit 3-1 may be done quantitatively. It will require inquiry, estimation, and inference to do so, but the process is enlightening in that it provides both knowledge and insights into areas where knowledge is absent. The latter portion of Exhibit 3-1, dealing with the strategic posture of each firm, generally calls for qualitative rather than quantitative assessment. Terms such as mission, objectives, and goals are used merely as guides to ensure that all that is known about the competitors' strategic postures will be spelled out.

42

EXHIBIT 3-1

Strategic Position Summary:
Metal Containers for Consumer Products

Strategic factors	American Can Company	Crown Cork & Seal	Others
Corporate Factors			
Financial Position			
Capital structure			
P/E multiple			
Cash flow			
etc.			
Executive Positions			
Risk posture			
Breadth of experience			
etc.			
Business Unit Factors			
Financial Analysis			
Ratios of performance			
Cash flow			
etc.			
Marketing System			
Product line/segments			
Distribution			
Product R&D			
etc.			
Research & Development			
Product (basic and applied)			
Process (basic and applied)			
Manufacturing Process			
Automation			
Capacity utilization			
Process R&D			
etc.			
Organizational and Human Resources			
Skill levels			
Wage rates			
Available supply			
Managers' objectives			
etc.			
Materials Position			
Quantity			
Price/quality			
etc.			cont.

Competitors

43

EXHIBIT 3-1 cont.

Strategic Position Summary:
Metal Containers for Consumer Products

Strategic factors	Competitors		
	American Can Company	Crown Cork & Seal	Others
External Relationships			
Regulatory rules			
International trade position			
etc.			
Summary of Each Firm's Strategic Posture			
Mission			
Objectives			
Strategy			
Strategic Programs			
Goals			

The analyst should write a brief synopsis of the strategy that is being pursued by each competitor. If any of a competitor's functional strategies seem to be inconsistent with the general strategy being pursued, the analyst must seek to determine which of the following possible explanations is most accurate:

1. Is the competition completing an alteration of its strategy, but the last one or two functions have not been modified to the point of being consistent with the other elements?
2. Is the competitor in a static strategic position with one or two factors that are not supportive and thus reduce the strength of its position? If so, how quickly can deficiencies be remedied?
3. Has the analyst made a mistake in the assessment of the competitor's position or action? What additional cost-effective data sources are available?
4. Is the competitor beginning to shift its traditional strategy with respect to this market, and if so, in which direction does it seem to be moving?

Overall Strategic Position Assessment

A business unit's position in its industry may be assessed in terms of a business screening matrix such as that shown in Exhibit 3-2. The business unit should be located in one of the nine elements of the

EXHIBIT 3-2

Business Screening Matrix

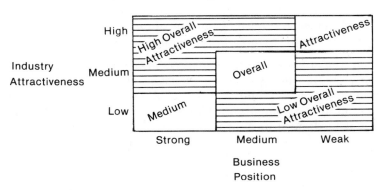

matrix according to the attractiveness of the industry in which it participates (as depicted by the rows of the matrix) and its position of relative strength in the industry (as depicted by the columns).

The *business screen*, popularized by General Electric,[1] is a descriptive device with evaluative and normative strategy implications. Locating an industry in one of the three rows requires consideration of a wide range of factors, such as:

Market size and growth potential
Competitive structure
Financial and economic factors
Technological factors
Social and political factors

Locating a business unit's position in one of the columns requires that its size, market share, and comparative advantages in all areas be assessed through the methods described in this and the remaining chapters of this section.[2]

The three areas of the matrix labeled low, medium, and high overall attractiveness reflect the evaluative implications of this assessment. Businesses located in the lower right have low overall attractiveness because they have relatively weak positions in relatively unattractive industries. In the upper left, business units have relatively strong positions in relatively attractive industries.

Developing a Business Screen

The business screen of Exhibit 3-2 reflects the results of a process that must be conducted in the business unit. The process involves two primary phases:

1. Identifying the factors that are relevant in determining industry attractiveness and business unit position
2. Determining the nature of the overall relationship of these factors

Thus, the judgment of the managers of the business unit may hold that an attractive industry has specific market, competitive, financial, technological, social, and political characteristics. Once this judgment is made, assessments must be combined into an overall ranking. This may be done on an entirely subjective basis or through the use of a weighting scheme such as those that have been developed for new product evaluations[3] and R&D project selection.[4]

For instance, if the managers decide to use only six broad factors to assess industry attractiveness, they might rate each factor on a zero to one scale and weight the importance of each factor by dividing 100 points among them. Exhibit 3-3 shows how such a weighting scheme might be performed. Column A indicates the score assigned to each factor on a zero to one scale. The importance weight of each factor is shown in Column B. The last column indicates the products of the other columns, and these are added to arrive at a total score, which in this example is forty-nine. This total score has meaning when compared with similar rankings of other industries using the same factors. It may be used as a basis for locating an industry in one of the three rows of Exhibit 3-2.

EXHIBIT 3-3

Industry Attractiveness Evaluation:
An Illustration

Industry factors	A Attractiveness score	B Importance weight	A x B Overall score	
Market Size	0.5	30	15.0	
Growth	0.1	20	2.0	
Competition	0.8	10	8.0	
Financial	0.4	20	8.0	
Technology	0.6	10	6.0	
Social-political	1.0	10	10.0	
		100	49.0	Total Score

EXHIBIT 3-4

Business Screen Depicting
Strategy Possibilities

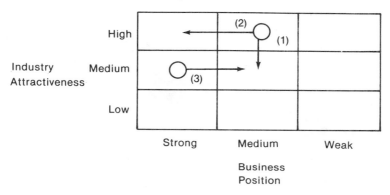

Using the Business Screen

The normative implications of the business screen can be seen if one considers the changes in the position of business units that might be effected by strategy changes. Some of these have been depicted on the business screening matrix in Exhibit 3-4. (The numbers below correspond to the numbered arrows in Exhibit 3-4.)

1. Invest to hold position (in a market of declining attractiveness)
2. Invest to improve position (shown for a highly attractive industry)
3. Harvest (shown for a situation in which a strong position is exchanged for cash)

Assessing a Business Unit's Prospects
for Forward or Backward Integration

Industry attractiveness is treated as a fixed element when one is using the business screen model. However, among the possible strategies for a business unit, forward and backward integration into other segments of the overall industrial production process are natural considerations. An assessment of the role played by the business unit in its industrial process is essential both to understanding its position and to considering possible strategic changes in that position.

EXHIBIT 3-5

Value-added Stages of an Industry Sector

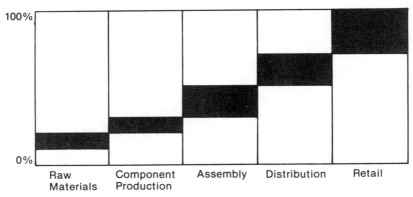

Value-added Considerations

The incentives that adjacent participants in an industry see in possible forward or backward integration to upset the existing market structure will be influenced by the distribution of value-added between the raw material supplier and the final consumer and the comparative advantages of different participants across functions. In Exhibit 3-5, for example, an efficient manufacturer of components might be tempted to shift forward if the assembler seems to be inefficient. On the other hand, the small value-added in the component production stage probably does not seem very attractive to those in the assembly stage.

Viewed from the perspective of competitors, such an assessment can have defensive implications as well. A high value-added position adjacent to a strong customer, as might be the case with a supplier to a giant retailer such as Sears, Roebuck, could mean a lack of opportunity for flexibility in the manufacturer's strategy and the ever-present danger of backward integration from the retailer.[5]

Mobility Barriers

The concept of entry barriers, factors inhibiting entry by a new business into a segment of an industry, has been generalized to that of mobility barriers. This idea holds that the difficulty of entry into an industry depends on the strategic position that a firm seeks to adopt. Mobility barriers are the deterrents to a shift in the strategic position of a firm in an industry and factors that give some firms advantages over others.[6] Such barriers can be described in terms of:[7]

48

1. Economies of scale
2. Product differentiation
3. Capital requirements
4. Cost disadvantages independent of size
5. Access to distribution channels
6. Government policy

Economies of scale   Scale economies force a potential entrant into a new business sector to enter on a large scale or accept the unit cost disadvantages that are inherent in low production volume. Such economies may also exist in research, marketing, distribution, financing, or other parts of a business.

Product differentiation   A strong product identification creates customer loyalty, which forces new entrants to spend heavily to overcome the loyalty. Thus this entry barrier may be significant in a business in which products are clearly differentiated one from another.

Capital requirements   The need to expend large sums "up front" to enter a business is a clear barrier to entry. Capital may be required not only for physical facilities, but for R&D, advertising, credit, inventories, and other costs.

Cost disadvantages independent of size   Firms already in an industry often have cost advantages that are the result of their history rather than their size. For instance, proprietary technology, existing relationships with suppliers, favorable location, and existing assets all may favor entrenched firms over new entrants.

Access to distribution channels   If distribution channels are limited in any way, the entrant may face a barrier so difficult that it may require the development of entirely new channels.

Government policy   License requirements, environmental and safety regulations, and a variety of other government actions can serve to give entrenched firms significant advantages over prospective entrants.

If a business is considering expansion of its role across the stages of an industry sector, it must consider the value-added opportunities as well as the entry or mobility barriers to forward or backward integration strategies. Only when the opportunity has been determined to be significant and the barriers have been shown to be manageable does such a move make sense.

49

Summary

This chapter sets the stage for Chapters 4–8 in that it develops ideas and methods that will serve as a basis for assessing the overall position of a business unit in a preliminary fashion.

The assessment is preliminary because it can be, and usually is, done without benefit of the more detailed functional analyses that are discussed in Chapters 4–7.

The methods of this chapter are aimed at clarifying the concept of comparative advantage, providing an overall framework within which the more detailed functional-level assessments should subsequently be made, and establishing the overall position of the business unit in a preliminary way that can subsequently be reviewed and revised.

Chapters 4–7 provide the methods for performing more detailed functional analyses. In Chapter 8, we then return to the overall level to deal with revisions and with assessments that can only be made as a consequence of the functional-level analyses.

Notes

1. "General Electric's 'Stoplight Strategy' for Planning," *Business Week*, April 28, 1975, p. 49.

2. See also W. E. Rothschild, *Putting It All Together: A Guide to Strategic Thinking* (New York: AMACOM, 1976).

3. William R. King, *Quantitative Analysis for Marketing Management* (New York: McGraw-Hill, 1967), chapter 5.

4. William R. King and D. I. Cleland, *Strategic Planning and Policy* (New York: Van Nostrand Reinhold, 1978).

5. For an example of some of the possible difficulties with such a position, see "Easco: Turning to New Customers While Helping Sears Promote Tools," *Business Week*, October 6, 1980, p. 66.

6. R. E. Caves and M. E. Porter, "From Entry Barriers to Mobility Barriers: Conjectural Decisions and Contrived Deterrence to New Competition," *Quarterly Journal of Economics*, May, 1977, pp. 241-261.

7. M. E. Porter, "How Competitive Forces Shape Strategy," *Harvard Business Review*, March-April, 1979, pp. 137-145.

CHAPTER 4

Financial Aspects
of Strategy Analysis

THIS CHAPTER extends the overall analysis of Chapter 2 into the financial domain. It also further extends the internal analysis activity shown on the left side of Exhibits 2-3 and 2-5 (for the integrated and diversified firms respectively). As in the previous chapter, the terminology of the business unit will generally be used, although all ideas are equally appropriate to the corporate level of an integrated firm.

The analysis of financial statements is common practice for investors and creditors, but their purposes are usually different from those of an analyst who is seeking to interpret and assess the strategy of a firm. In this chapter, we develop some of the financial concepts that can be useful in understanding the implications of strategic options.* We also suggest ways in which these same tools can help in decoding the behavior of competitors. Finally, we consider such specific financial analyses as product line profitability, capacity expansion, tax analysis, and return on investment (ROI) analysis.

There are two major difficulties that must be addressed in any financial analyses to be used for strategic purposes—the effects of inflation and aggregation. This chapter presumes that the reader is aware of these difficulties.

Product Line Profitability

In most instances, the first analysis required to gain an understanding of the economic characteristics of an individual business unit or

---

* This chapter presumes that the reader is familiar with basic financial concepts and calculations such as those presented in Leopold A. Bernstein, *Financial Statement Analysis* (Homewood, Illinois: R. D. Irwin, 1978).

51

product line is some form of product line profitability analysis. (See Chapter 5 for an operational description of product lines.) If it does not know which of its products actually earned profits, a firm can easily orient its strategy in an inappropriate direction. The problem is especially acute in firms that sell related or complementary products and services, because there is a natural tendency for a production-oriented firm to overlook customers' primary interests. For example, two adjoining automotive service stations may find themselves engaged in a price war because one station wishes to sell large volumes of fuel at a low price while the other views gasoline as a means of attracting customers for its repair shop. Similar problems arise with retail banks which may not be able to recognize and treat such services as convenient check-cashing, rapid loan processing, and accessible safe deposit boxes as separate entities that deserve individual analysis and attention.

In extreme cases, firms may discover that they have carelessly broadened their product lines or added helpful services to the point where primary products can no longer be handled efficiently. There are so many exceptions that buyers begin to expect customized service. In short, product line analyses not only focus attention on short-term questions of margins and return on investment; they also offer secondary benefits by stimulating the refinement of marketing strategy.

Preparing the Product Line Analysis

The preparation of product line profitability analyses begins with the process of separating revenue, expense, and investment categories in accordance with the level of detail desired in the study. One could, for example, analyze a category such as food items or pursue more detail by studying beverages, or soft drinks, or Brand X. Analyses inevitably become more expensive and typically become more arbitrary with each additional level of detail. This arbitrariness comes from the need to allocate the cost of shared facilities and services (such as production plants and computer support) to multiple product lines. As a second step, one should try to separate variable expenses from those of a more fixed nature, so that the fluctuation of profits in relationship to sales volume can be readily determined.

Exhibit 4-1 shows an illustrative product line analysis for three product lines labeled A, B, and C. In preparation of such an analysis, the paramount concern must be the identification of controllable elements of strategy. For instance, although we deliberately set out the *discretionary* expenses separately in Exhibit 4-1, there are firms in

EXHIBIT 4-1

Product Line Profitability Analysis

	A		B		C		Total
	$	%	$	%	$	%	($)
Sales units	1,000		10,000		100		11,100
Sales price	×100		×10		×1,000		27.02
Gross revenues	100,000	100	100,000	100	100,000	100	300,000
Direct expenses:							
Material	−15,000	−15	−15,000	−15	−25,000	−25	−55,000
Labor	−25,000	−25	−10,000	−10	−10,000	−10	−45,000
Overhead (variable)	−10,000	−10	−5,000	−5	−5,000	−5	−20,000
Gross margin	50,000	50	70,000	70	60,000	60	180,000
Variable selling, general, and administrative expenses	−10,000	−10	−30,000	−30	−20,000	−20	−60,000
Marginal contributions	40,000	40	40,000	40	40,000	40	120,000
Fixed expenses	−10,000	−10	−10,000	−10	−15,000	−15	−35,000
Discretionary expenses	−5,000	−5	-0-	-0-	−10,000	−10	−15,000
Allocated expenses	−10,000	−10	−10,000	−10	−10,000	−10	−30,000
Income before taxes	15,000	15	20,000	20	5,000	5	40,000
Income taxes (50%)	−7,500	−7.5	−10,000	−10	−2,500	−2.5	−20,000
Income after taxes	7,500	7.5	10,000	10	2,500	2.5	20,000
Investment (net)	50,000		10,000		50,000		110,000
Return on investment	15%		100%		5%		18%
Capacity utilization rate	50%		80%		70%		n/a

which these are "buried" in a single "Selling, General, and Administrative Expense" (SG&A) category. A failure to distinguish those expenses necessary to maintain current operations from those invested to ameliorate an area of weakness or to develop an arena of strength can undermine a business's capacity to understand the relationship between its strategic intentions and its cash outlays. For example, advertising outlays can often be divided into two classes: those featuring the weekly specials, which stimulate current sales, and those emphasizing the product's convenience, friendliness, or quality, which are intended to enhance long-term image or attract new market segments. In the same way, R&D expenses should be segregated between those devoted to solving warranty problems and those aimed at capturing future market opportunities. Because managers can exercise considerable influence over discretionary expenses, they reflect the mechanisms through which changes in strategic posture can be implemented.

Precisely because the information content of such breakdowns is so high, there are obvious incentives to aggregate such data for external reporting purposes. Nonetheless, strategists who are interested in simultaneously measuring short-term profitability of subunits and monitoring the direction of movement in their strategic postures must have a means of determining the consistency of such factors as discretionary expenses over time, so that strategic moves are not subverted by the predictable "quarterly profit squeeze."

The detailed components of the variable selling, general, and administrative (VSG&A) expense category can include everything from sales commissions to warranty expenses, so the first analysis required with most product lines is the division of expenses according to activity, such as selling, collection, and supplies. It then becomes possible to evaluate a proposal to modify a distribution and delivery system or to improve product design and tighten the quality assurance standards in order to reduce warranty expense. In some instances, well-intentioned proposals to "improve our products" or "cut warranty expenses" are simply not apt to be justifiable in terms of the economic tradeoffs. On the other hand, in those organizations not bound by tight economic constraints, a decision to sell only "top quality merchandise" can at least be evaluated in terms of the potential profit lost in the pursuit of such an objective.

What-If? Product Line Analyses

To make strategic use of product line profitability analyses, one may ask a series of "What-if?" questions. For instance, in Exhibit 4-1, if an additional $20,000 of discretionary expense in two equal amounts over the next two years could increase sales of Product Line A to 80 percent of capacity in two steps, then income after taxes would rise from $7,500 to $8,500 and then $14,500. If investment remained constant, such an increase in capacity utilization would increase return on investment (ROI) to 29 percent from 15 percent. Attempting to reach the same ROI objective by controlling expenses, rather than increasing sales during the second year, would have re-

54

quired a reduction of $14,000 in pretax expenses during that year—an amount equal to almost three times the original discretionary expense level of $5,000 and thus almost impossible to obtain.

Product Line B shows an impressive ROI of 100 percent, but there is not much opportunity to expand sales without adding capacity. The additional capital required to expand this product line is quite trivial, but with a variable selling, general, and administrative expense of 30 percent, it is apparent that considerable marketing effort would be required to achieve these levels. The major question for Product Line B must necessarily focus on the cost of additional market penetration.

The situation with Product Line C raises different strategic issues. For example, has the $10,000 of discretionary expense, perhaps for R&D, yielded any insights into possible product improvement or materials cost reduction? If we totally eliminated this expenditure, would our position be threatened as ROI rose to 15 percent? On the other hand, if there is little expansion or growth expected for what might be a mature product, is it possible to liquidate part of the investment? If $10,000 of investment could be sold and $1,000 of depreciation thus eliminated, the ROI could be raised from 5 percent to 7½ percent through such a disinvestment move.

Trend Analysis of Product Line Profitability

An important extension of the preceding static product line analysis involves the trended or time-series data, which also deserve examination. By analyzing inflation-adjusted data over a period of years, the strategist can determine which aspects of a product line have eroded and which have been susceptible to strengthening from particular initiatives. Changes in position, of course, must be examined in the context of rivals' behavior and managerial action (or inaction). For example, gross margin may erode because of increasing competition, careless pricing practices, or uncontrollable direct cost increases. In the final analysis, the most important conclusions from these studies separate industry-wide phenomena from those that are unique to a given firm and then distinguish the controllable actions from the uncontrollable events. It is only at such a point that decisions can be made regarding SBU positioning.

Sensitivity Analysis of Product Line Costs

After trends have been examined for a given product line, it is then time to begin an evaluation of relationships among performance measures in the product line profitability analysis. There is always a temptation to examine carefully the large expense categories, such as labor for Product A or material for Product C, but it is equally important to be concerned with modest changes that might yield a higher markup or a lower spoilage rate. The small steps that yield increased efficiency may be very critical to a firm's overall economic health, particularly in relatively mature markets. The basic question, however, must be "Do our internal financial analyses reflect adherence to the existing strategy for this product line?"

Changes in product line sales dollars, for example, must be divided into price and volume factors, so that changes in market price sensitivity can be distinguished from levels of market penetration. It is not uncommon to have changes in relative product or service quality disguised in the income statement because volume has moved in the opposite direction from unit price.

Within the direct expense category, shifts in the proportion of sales dollars devoted to materials or labor can point to problems or special opportunities. Rising direct material ratios in a paperboard box plant could signify a deliberate choice to upgrade the quality of finished boxes, an uncontrollable increase in paper prices, or careless production methods that resulted in wasted materials. In short, the observation of changes in direct material ratios might confirm a desired change in strategy or might be an early indicator of an eroding control system in a manufacturing facility. Similarly, direct labor costs may be expected to rise because of a decision to increase the quality of craftsmanship in a product, or they may decline because of an investment in more automatic machinery or a streamlined facilities layout.

The internal consistency of a product-market strategy aimed at moving a product line to a higher price through increasing quality can be explicitly tested in this way. If unit prices have increased as much or more than direct material and labor have risen, it is probably fair to assume that the strategy has been effectively implemented— assuming, of course, that there has not been an unexpectedly disastrous decline in volume.

Relating Various Product Line Expense Elements

To further evaluate strategy, it is useful to relate analyses such as those of the variable selling, general, and administrative expenses to the indicators of direct production expenses. For example, the cost of advertising and selling a certain quantity of a product line is a function of the quality of the units manufactured as it compares to that of the competition's product. A superbly efficient conversion process

56

will make it much easier to keep marketing expenses below industry standards. Conversely, a strategic decision to produce mediocre goods or services in an aging facility may demand both price concessions and extra marketing pressure in order to maintain a profitable position in the face of competitors with higher quality products or services. Because the array of feasible combinations of production technologies and selling and administrative procedures is so great, it becomes extremely important for the manager to continuously monitor the relationships between the two sets of cost elements.

Capacity Expansion Analysis

In order to illustrate the role that the analysis of fixed costs can play in the strategic planning for a business line, consider the breakeven analysis shown in Exhibit 4-2. The manager of Alpha Product foresees that sales of the rapidly growing product line may exceed capacity in Year T. However, because of evolutions in technology, the most efficient incremental unit will more than double capacity, moving it

EXHIBIT 4-2

Profitability Analysis
for Capacity Expansion

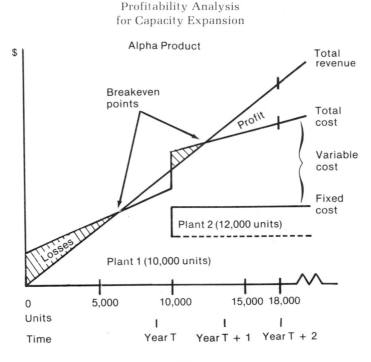

57

from 10,000 to 22,000 units per year. As a result of the related jump in fixed costs, Alpha may actually show a loss for part of Year T, since operating profits may not reach the preexpansion level until Year T + 1. On the other hand, if the parent corporation is willing to recognize the possible strategic importance of adding only efficient capacity increments in a rapidly expanding market, Alpha will be in a position to reach a ROI level equal to full capacity in Plant 1 when Plant 2 is at only about two-thirds capacity. (Obviously, a number of simplifying assumptions have been made regarding depreciation rates, unit prices, and similar factors, but the essential need to sacrifice short-term profits in order to capture the benefits of lower variable expenses per unit of production is valid.)

Depending on the particular firm within which Alpha Product is attempting to grow, the dramatic expansion may be viewed in different ways. A firm that relies heavily on Alpha for its profits may choose a smaller, relatively inefficient increment of capacity in order to avoid the visible losses from the surge of expenses in advance of rising sales. Another firm, which may have several similarly growing product lines, may be most concerned about sequencing the expansions so that cash flow and profitability measures for the corporation taken as a whole do not deteriorate. In most instances, however, there will be some bends in the total revenue curve as unit prices change in response to oversupply or undersupply situations during periods of plant expansions.

Some firms may miss an opportunity even to consider this important financial aspect of strategic choice because the product line manager's performance may be measured so heavily on monthly profits that he or she will pretend that "market growth is limited" in order not to risk having to explain the loss of profits during the expansion process. Unfortunately, the myopia will not become obvious until market position begins to deteriorate and price pressures eventually take their toll on margins. The "clever" product manager may then be tempted to reduce discretionary expenses in order to sustain profitability, and the vicious cycle of product line deterioration will almost be complete.

Tax Analyses

Unlike many of the financial dimensions noted thus far, tax calculations often receive relatively little attention at the business unit level. "Taxes are a corporate problem!" is the response one often hears from division managers. However, because many forms of property, wage, and sales taxes are levied at the local level, decisions regarding facility locations must consider the impact of taxes on the relative competitive strength of the resulting operations. Further, structural designs may be influenced by applicable investment tax credits, depreciation rates, and other available incentives. Income tax rates, though usually viewed as being "the same across the board," may vary substantially when a business is under a tax holiday provision in an offshore location. Consequently, performance evaluations made for a business unit on an after-tax basis may seem very favorable, but the resulting cash flow may not be available for remission to corporate headquarters for several years unless a penalty or *"tollgate"* tax is paid. Depending on the geographical and timing distributions of a firm's cash requirements, such local reinvestment incentives may or may not adversely influence the strategy of a firm at the corporate level.

Thus, the impact of different tax structures on business unit profitability analyses can vary widely and for many different reasons. At a minimum, it is essential to distinguish continuing from one-shot incentives and then to determine whether or not there are secondary consequences for the mobility of capital as a result of any special benefits.

Return on Investment Analysis

Though long a favorite summary performance measure among analysts and managers alike, return on investment (ROI) must be treated carefully when it is used to evaluate or interpret an operating unit's performance. In addition to summarizing the varied treatments afforded its dozens of components, ROI is a ratio that can be calculated several different ways:

1. $\text{ROI} = \dfrac{\text{Income after tax}}{\text{Total assets}}$ or $\dfrac{\text{IAT}}{\text{TA}}$

2. $\text{ROI} = \dfrac{\text{IAT (without extraordinary items)}}{\text{Net assets or TA less current liabilities}}$ or $\dfrac{\text{IAT}}{\text{TA-CL}}$

3. $\text{ROI} = \dfrac{\text{Income before tax}}{\text{TA-CL}}$ or $\dfrac{\text{IBT}}{\text{TA-CL}}$

4. $\text{ROI} = \dfrac{\text{IAT}}{\text{Current value}}$ or $\dfrac{\text{IAT}}{\text{CV}}$

59

Challenges emerge in the interpretation of each of the different definitions of ROI, so it behooves strategists to be sure that they understand the relationships between business unit objectives and the form of measuring stick to be applied. ROI calculated in the first way might encourage a manager to add personnel rather than equipment because "people don't appear on the books." A tendency to experience raw material shortages with definition (1) may disappear with formula (2) or formula (3) because in the latter instances the manager receives credit for unpaid trade credit in the calculation.

Calculation (4) represents an effort to integrate historical performance (IAT) with future prospects (current value). Because of the widely recognized difficulties of separating IAT into operating profits, holding gains, and inflationary effects, along with the costly or subjective processes involved in determining current value, measures such as these have not been widely used. Nonetheless, as strategists seek economically logical resource allocation criteria, increasing attention must be paid to the quality and the frequency of the indicators used.[1]

In recognition of the dysfunctional consequences that often result from the broad application of overly generalized criteria, some firms have begun to use measures of net contributed income or residual income to evaluate the dollar value of a business's contributions above some imputed cost of capital. Such measures have been of particular interest to older diversified firms that have experienced difficulty shifting away from capital intensive industries with low profitability. By rewarding managers for contributions (or pure profits) above the firm's average after-tax cost of capital, many firms have found that business unit managers in high return (and often high growth) markets are willing to invest more aggressively and sacrifice short-term ROI. As we shall see in later chapters, providing constructive management incentives for moving resources among business sectors becomes a very critical activity in aggressive, multimarket firms.

Cash Flow Analysis

The analysis of financial aspects of a business unit's strategic posture is not complete without some attention to the critical dimension of cash flow. Depending on the liquidity position of a firm, the *cash management function* may attract a greater or lesser degree of top management attention. However, all too many firms have belatedly discovered that their inattention to cash flow patterns has permitted them to accumulate inventories, neglect accounts receivable, or let cash stand idle when more profitable opportunities existed. As well, some aggressive managers have failed to recognize the inflexibility and time-consuming negotiations that may result from overinvesting in assets with negative short-term cash flows.[2]

Just as managers seek to maintain cash flow flexibility so that they can respond efficiently to new opportunities or unanticipated problems, competitors are prone to analyze the capacity of a firm to respond financially to a major new facilities expansion or related initiative.[3] In some extreme instances, the effectiveness of cash flow management has determined whether a given firm remained an independent firm or was acquired in a hostile takeover. Many firms have purchased large quantities of treasury stock to reduce their *liquid asset visibility* or to recover a large minority block from a hostile shareholder. In these and many other ways, cash flows play critical roles in the strategic planning function of almost all corporations.

Summary

Financial analyses are among the most commonly performed analyses in modern business. However, they are often performed for reasons that are not strategic in nature. This chapter treats those financial analysis concepts and methods that are most useful for assessing the strategic position of the business unit.

Notes

1. A. Rappaport, "Executive Incentives Versus Corporate Growth," *Harvard Business Review*, July-August, 1978, pp. 81–88; P. F. Drucker, "Learning from Foreign Management," *Wall Street Journal*, June 4, 1980; and Carol J. Loomis, "How GE Manages Inflation," *Fortune*, May 4, 1981, pp. 121–124.

2. Pearson Hunt, "Funds Position: Keystone in Financial Position," *Harvard Business Review*, May-June, 1975, pp. 106–115.

3. For further discussion of the criticality of cash flows, see William Fruhan, Jr., "Pyrrhic Victories in Fights for Market Share," *Harvard Business Review*, September-October, 1972, pp. 100–107 and his *Financial Strategy* (Homewood, Illinois: R. D. Irwin, 1979).

CHAPTER 5

Marketing Aspects
of Strategy Analysis

THIS CHAPTER continues the elaboration of the internal analysis element of the planning frameworks of Exhibits 2-3 and 2-5 as they apply to the assessment of the marketing aspects of strategy. As in Chapters 3 and 4, the level of analysis is the business unit in which the search for comparative advantage is extended to the domain of marketing.

The analysis and identification of comparative advantage from among marketing variables requires growth-share matrix analysis, market segmentation, product line and product life cycle analysis, and distribution system analysis.

Growth-Share Matrix Analysis

A major analytic framework for depicting one's overall market position relative to competition is the growth-share matrix.[1] Analyses based on growth-share matrices enhance one's ability both to evaluate a current position and to plan future strategy.

To use the growth-share matrix, a firm must have the ability to estimate the approximate rate of growth of the market as well as its own position in the market. As shown in Exhibit 5-1, four (or more) categories are identified in terms of these two dimensions:

Stars—Product lines in a high growth rate sector and with a strong market position in that sector

Dogs—Product lines in a low growth rate sector and with a weak position in that sector

Cash Cows—Product lines in a low growth rate sector, having a strong position in that sector

EXHIBIT 5-1

Growth-Share Matrix

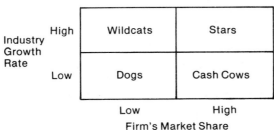

Wildcats—Product lines in a high growth rate sector, but having a weak position in that sector

The growth-share matrix suggests the nature of expected competition under each of the four circumstances. For example, a firm with a high market share in a rapidly growing industry can hope to have a highly profitable star *if* it is able to maintain the necessary investment to retain market share and fulfill market volume requirements. Such a position is usually very costly for others to attack, because cost advantages and brand recognition favor the major firm in a growing market.

In sharp contrast to the star position is that of the dogs. Such product lines have probably been squeezed into a position of only marginal profitability, and the path to greater market power is expected to be very costly because increased market share can only come at the expense of other competitors. Hence, the incentives are very strong for horizontal acquisitions, innovations that will redefine the market, or liquidation.

Thus, clear strategic implications come from the positioning of a product line in one of the four categories in the growth-share matrix. If one goes further to examine how a competitor might assess the situation differently, the strategic implications are enriched further. For instance, suppose one assumes that most competitors would be in reasonable agreement as to the location of the industry on the vertical axis—the expected industry growth rate. If one firm's perceptions of an industry's future growth rate differ significantly, however, the prospects for strategic rivalry are high. For example, a large competitor that foresees growth rates as low may begin to "milk" what it feels is a cash cow, removing cash by minimizing reinvestment. In contrast, a somewhat smaller rival that is more optimistic about the industry's growth rates may begin to invest heavily to shift its wildcat into the star category.

63

Thus, a growth-share matrix analysis can provide the basis for establishing the competitive position of a product line as well as for assessing strategies that might create comparative advantage.

The similarities between the growth-share matrix of Exhibit 5-1 and the business screen analysis discussed in Chapter 3 should be noted at this point. The two are similar but not identical. The growth-share matrix is a concept that deals with market phenomena (share and growth rate), while the business screen is an overall evaluative device. The processes for developing the two are also different in that the location of a product on the growth-share matrix is more objectively assessable than is the location of an SBU on the business screen matrix. The reader should return to Chapter 3 to review the weighting procedure described there for the business screen and compare that procedure with the relatively simple assessments required for the growth-share matrix.

Market Segmentation and Product Line Analysis

Market segments are portions of an overall market; they may be defined in various ways, such as by geography or the characteristics of the consumers in each segment. The strategic purpose in segmenting a market is usually to achieve some comparative advantage within one or more segments through product design, pricing, or other factors. For example, various automobile models may compete with rivals in some segments in terms of price and fuel economy while at the same time competing with others in terms of safety and performance. This differential basis for competition may be supported by product line variations (for example, a basic product may be given added features to make it appeal to a given consumer group), or it may be primarily supported through different advertising appeals, different prices, and other nonproduct variables. Thus, when automobile manufacturers create a sports model by adding racing stripes, larger tires, and paint options to a basic model, they are modifying the product to gain special advantage in a market segment that has been identified to be responsive to these features. Similarly, when prices are cut on some models, or when they are advertised with different appeals in different regions of the nation or world, different market segments are being addressed using nonproduct variables.

When market segments are identified and differentially addressed, a *product line* is naturally created. The various products in the line may be physically distinct, packaged distinctively, or merely promoted and sold on different bases.

64

In any case, the segmentation of a market poses difficult tradeoffs in terms of the breadth of a firm's product line. The strategic problems arising from such product line decisions have been summarized by Barbara Jackson and Benson Shapiro:

> A (product) line longer than needed, on the one hand, faces high costs from increased inventory, production changeovers, and additional order processing and transportation. An overly long line also creates confusion in marketing to distributors, salespeople, and customers.
>
> An overly short line, on the other hand, results in different cost problems. Potential losses include sales, competitive position, and economies of scale. Distributors and salespeople may reduce their marketing effort.
>
> The financial impacts of either type mistake are clear. The organizational impacts arise because the costs of the two types of mistake are felt most heavily by separate parts of the organization. . . .[2]

The objective of market segmentation is the creation of comparative advantage. A consequence of any successful market segmentation is the erection of varying barriers to entry for prospective new entrants.

Although *barriers to entry* are often described in terms of manufacturing plant size, patent protection, and capital requirements, marketing dimensions often offer the most severe strategic challenges. An automobile produced abroad may face its greatest challenge in securing a national sales and service network here, while a small beverage company may be thwarted by the cost of gaining brand recognition or retail shelf space.

Each marketing barrier will have a different level of effectiveness against each prospective new competitor. There are many attributes of an industry that can create strategic entry barriers. The nature of available product or service substitutes will influence the effectiveness of segmentation and barrier construction. If the product has numerous technical equivalents so that substitutes are readily available, perceived image and price may be the only feasible barriers.

On the other hand, carefully and laboriously constructed barriers may be overcome by creative substitutes. For instance, one service-conscious firm supplying the electrical utility industry spent a decade establishing a reliable national network of service centers to ensure rapid maintenance at its major installations—clearly a competitive advantage that could not be supplanted quickly. Surprising to the diligent firm, however, was a competitor's response in the form of air cargo and jet age mechanics. Customers did not seem to mind paying premium prices for fast service when they were told that "everything had to be flown in." Thus, the analysis of inventory storage and maintenance costs and customer price sensitivity provided the basis for a strategic response that was implemented in ten weeks to overcome a barrier that took ten years to construct.[3]

In some product areas, there may be no ready substitutes. Rock music groups, supersonic airliners, and other products may provide opportunities for monopolistic pricing practices, but, as with so many strategic weapons, such pricing may have both positive and negative results. If the price is not high enough, the service or product may not be seen as being unique, but if it is too high, it will create strong pressures for the creation of substitutes or the acceptance of alternatives.

As more firms refine their concepts of market segmentation, the flexibility of prices is apt to increase. Dow Chemical is a firm that has established a reputation for moving prices up and down aggressively in response to demand and materials costs as it seeks to increase the profitability of its product lines.[4] A different form of flexibility has been displayed by some marketers of large industrial systems who, for example, have been willing to accept very thin margins on initial installations in order to secure the more lucrative long-term service contracts.

Product Life Cycle Analysis

Product life cycle (PLC) concepts have had substantial impacts on the ways in which most managers have for many years visualized competition. The PLC idea postulates that there are several phases in the life of a product and that each of these phases requires different varieties and levels of competitive effort.

Exhibit 5-2 shows the rate of generation of sales revenue slowly rising after a product is introduced (the development phase), rising rapidly thereafter (the growth phase), reaching a plateau (the maturation phase), and finally decreasing (the declining sales phase). Most products display such dynamic characteristics, although some, such as novelty items, may go through the various phases very rapidly, and others, such as established commodities, may stretch out the life cycle over many decades.

PLC Strategic Implications

The strategic implications of the life cycle are fairly clear. For instance, one can expect a firm to concentrate on product refinement

66

EXHIBIT 5-2

Product Life Cycle

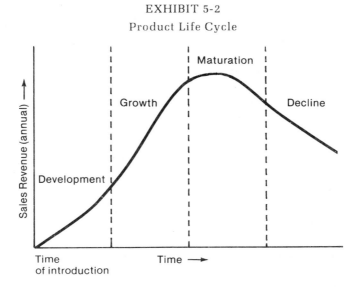

during the development phase and then shift emphasis to market share penetration during the growth phase. At a later point the focus might shift to manufacturing efficiencies in the maturity phase and cash flow generation during the decline. Indeed, all elements of effective product strategy may be related to the PLC. Product design, pricing, promotion and advertising, and distribution policy are strategy elements that may vary throughout the life cycle.

C. R. Wasson[5] has suggested that overall product strategy should evolve through a series of phases that are roughly equivalent to the phases of the life cycle:

1. To minimize learning requirements, locate and remedy offering defects quickly, develop widespread awareness of benefits, and gain trial by early adopters.
2. To establish a strong brand-market and distribution niche as quickly as possible.
3. To maintain and strengthen the market niche achieved through dealer and consumer loyalty.
4. To defend the position of a brand against competing brands and product category against other potential products, through constant attention to product improvement opportunities and fresh promotional and distribution approaches.
5. To milk the offering dry of all possible profit.

Similarly specific promotional objectives and media foci may vary in a sequence of steps throughout the life cycle to:

1. Create widespread awareness and understanding of offering benefits and gain trial by early adopters. This is done through use of publicity, personal sales, and mass communication.
2. Create and strengthen brand preference among the trade and final users and stimulate general trial. Use mass media, personal sales, sales promotions (including sampling), and publicity.
3. Maintain consumer franchise and strengthen dealer ties. The mass media emphasis continues, along with an increase in dealer-attracting sales promotions, personal selling to dealers, sales promotions, and publicity.
4. Maintain consumer and trade loyalty, with strong emphasis on dealers and distributors, and promote greater use frequency. The mass media and dealer-oriented promotions are used.
5. Phase out the advertising, keeping just enough to maintain profitable distribution. Cut down all media to the bone—use no sales promotions of any kind.

The strategy elements that come from the life cycle do not have to do solely with marketing. H. Fox[6] has provided hypotheses about appropriate strategies to follow in various functional areas throughout the life cycle. Following a series of life cycle phases ranging from precommercialization to decline, he suggests that the personnel strategy should involve this sequence:

1. Recruit for new activities; negotiate operational changes with unions.
2. Staff and train middle management; set up stock options for executives.
3. Add suitable personnel for the plant; expect many grievances and heavy overtime.
4. Make use of transfers, advancements, and incentives for efficiency, safety, and so on; set up a suggestion system.
5. Find new slots; encourage early retirement.

Charles Hofer has also developed an extensive set of contingencies that suggest the potentially fruitful uses for combinations of the various PLC phases with complementary actions in such areas as pricing, product development, and manufacturing investment.[7] David Rink has demonstrated ways in which sophisticated pricing concepts can help to extract even greater economic benefit from the PLC.[8]

Planned Life Cycles

The notion of the strategic implications of PLCs is a limited view of the ways in which the product life cycle can be used to strategic advantage. Life cycles need not be viewed as something imposed by the market; instead, they may be planned by the product's manufacturer.[9]

A product life cycle may be made more controllable and extended through a sequence of planned changes in the product. These changes can be thought of in product terms, market terms, or both. Developing variations of the basic product will enhance the likelihood of additional sales to existing customers; developing new product uses and appeals will increase the likelihood of demand by new customers. These two approaches are well illustrated by the product-market strategies of two photographic giants, Kodak and Polaroid. Kodak's introduction of refined versions of its pocket cameras, such as one with a built-in telephoto lens, is an example of product sequencing. Polaroid's introduction of lower-cost versions of its instant cameras is an illustration of market sequencing. In the Kodak case, the new version of the camera is designed to create additional customer satisfaction and product value by widening the potential use of pocket cameras, thus making the new versions appealing even to people who already own an earlier model. Polaroid, on the other hand, has usually followed a strategy of introducing the top of the line camera first and then successively introducing lower-cost versions in an attempt to appeal to new customer groups who could not afford the earlier versions.

The essence of both of these strategies is a planned sequence of product refinements which will maximize the benefits obtained from the basic product. In effect, these strategies extend the life cycle, as shown in Exhibit 5-3, through the addition of increments to the sales pattern as the basic product life cycle is in its maturation and declining sales phases.

Multiproduct Life Cycle Strategies

The idea of a multiproduct life cycle strategy is illustrated in Exhibit 5-4. This figure shows the anticipated revenue streams from three products over an eight-year period. In Exhibit 5-4, Product B is expected to begin producing revenues in 1986 and to enter the declining sales phase of its life cycle after 1990. Product A is already in the midst of a long declining sales phase. Under current plans, Product C is expected to be introduced in 1988.

The total revenue (the top curve in Exhibit 5-4) is predicted to go through a brief decrease in 1990 under this product life cycle strategy. If this is not consistent with the organization's objectives, as it would not be if the firm has the objective of constantly growing revenues,

69

EXHIBIT 5-3

Planned Product Life Cycle:
An Illustration

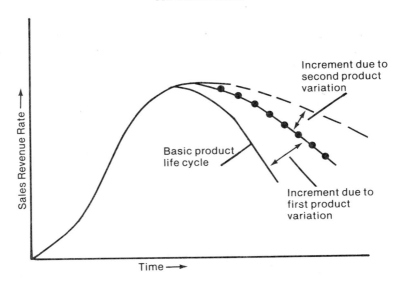

Source: William R. King and David I. Cleland, *Strategic Planning and Policy* (New York: Van Nostrand Reinhold Company, 1978), p. 178. With permission of publisher.

Product C's development may be speeded up. As an alternative, another new product may be considered for introduction about 1989. Or it may be necessary to go beyond the domain of new product development to design a strategy that will achieve the revenue objective; for instance, acquisitions may be considered.

Some PLC Caveats

In contrast to the enthusiasm that many analysts have shown for the PLC, others have suggested real difficulties in specifying market segments accurately enough to actually implement the PLC prescription in many actual situations.[10] G. Michael[11] and others have suggested refinements, such as the idea that the declining phase of the PLC may be different for various products. N. K. Dhalla and S. Yuspeh have gone so far as to argue for the abandonment of the PLC as a planning model,[12] but that polar position has not as yet received wide support. Cautious use and refinement of the PLC concept will probably continue, since it is easy to understand and has such clear strategy implications.

70

EXHIBIT 5-4
Multiproduct Life Cycle Strategy

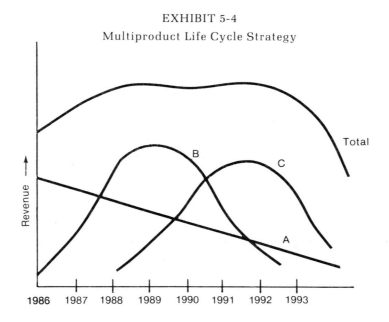

Distribution and Logistical Elements
of Strategy Analysis

Some of the most traditional aspects of overall marketing—physical distribution and logistics—are often not thought of as being relevent to strategy. However, these marketing subsystems can be strategically important when distribution costs are important or, as noted earlier, when innovative distribution methods such as air freight can be used to overcome traditional barriers to entry. For instance, one firm—a manufacturer of air conditioners—combined a distribution cost analysis with a forecast of the growth of demand for market segments in various geographic regions. This demonstrated that distribution of some of the products from the company's single production facility to certain areas of the country was likely to become uneconomical. Because air conditioners of certain types were most often purchased by certain end users (such as hospitals), the distribution cost analysis showed how the forecasted differential growth rates, combined with the distribution cost structure, could lead to future cost difficulties. As a result, the company adopted a strategy of planned cutback in the range of product models offered in certain geographic areas.[13]

71

Summary

The concept of the position of a business unit is often thought of in marketing terms. In Chapter 3, that concept was used broadly. In Chapter 8, the broad concept will again be addressed.

In this chapter, the idea of market position is addressed in terms of the growth-share matrix—a device that serves to define the role and potential of a business unit in market terms. This useful and much used approach provides a powerful, yet limited, description of a business unit in that it omits technology, manufacturing, and the other elements that define what a business is and what it can be. The chapter also treats market segmentation and product line and product life cycle analyses that are critical to the assessment of market position. It concludes with a brief discussion of some of the more traditional, and therefore often neglected, aspects of marketing—distribution and logistics—to illustrate their potential for strategic impact.

Notes

1. Originally popularized by the Boston Consulting Group in *Perspectives on Experience* (Boston: Boston Consulting Group, 1972).

2. Barbara B. Jackson and Benson P. Shapiro, "New Way to Make Product Line Decisions," *Harvard Business Review*, May-June, 1979, p. 140.

3. Additional insights into the role of logistics in the creation of strategy can be found in J. L. Heskett, "Logistics—Essential to Strategy," *Harvard Business Review*, November-December, 1977, pp. 85-96. The opposite of entry barriers can also be influential, as demonstrated in Kathryn R. Harrigan, "The Effect of Exit Barriers upon Strategic Flexibility," *Strategic Management Journal*, April-June, 1980, pp. 165-176.

4. "Flexible Pricing," *Business Week*, December 12, 1977, pp. 78-88.

5. C. R. Wasson, *Dynamic Competitive Strategy and Product Life Cycles* (Austin, Texas: Austin Press, 1978), pp. 256–257.

6. H. Fox, "A Framework for Functional Coordination," *Atlanta Economic Review*, November-December, 1973, pp. 10-11.

7. Charles W. Hofer, "Toward a Contingency Theory of Business Strategy," *Academy of Management Journal*, December, 1975, pp. 784-810.

8. David R. Rink, "A Theoretical Extension of the Product Life Cycle Concept," *Pittsburgh Business Review*, December, 1977, pp. 12-19.

9. T. Levitt, "Exploit the Product Life Cycle," *Harvard Business Review*, November-December, 1965, pp. 81-94; and C. R. Anderson and C. P. Zeitham, "Stage of Product Life Cycle as Determinant of Business Strategy: An Empirical Test Using PIMS Data," Academy of Management, San Diego, August, 1981.

10. George S. Day and Allan D. Shocker, "Identifying Competitive Product Market Boundaries: Strategic and Analytical Issues," Report #76-112 (Cambridge: Marketing Sciences Institute, 1976).

11. G. Michael, "Product Petrification: A New Stage in the Life Cycle," *California Management Review*, Fall, 1971, pp. 88-91.

12. N. K. Dhalla and S. Yuspeh, "Forget the Product Life Cycle Concept," *Harvard Business Review*, January-February, 1976, pp. 102-112.

13. J. L. Heskett, *op. cit.*

CHAPTER 6

Manufacturing Aspects
of Strategy Analysis

THIS CHAPTER continues to elaborate on the internal analysis element of the strategic planning framework outlined in Exhibit 2-3 and 2-5, looking into the domain of manufacturing. As in Chapters 3, 4, and 5, the discussion is focused on the business unit, although the analyses are equally applicable to the corporate level of an integrated firm.

Many organizations conceive and seek to implement strategies without giving adequate attention to the opportunities afforded by, and the constraints imposed by, manufacturing or other conversion processes.[1] New products are sometimes actually test marketed in limited areas before anyone knows if they can be manufactured or distributed efficiently in quantity.

To avoid such a lack of integration of manufacturing into overall strategy, the role of quality, perceived quality, and price must be understood. Then, analyses may be done in terms of comparative costs, experience curve effects, minimum efficient scale facilities, capacity utilization, and materials procurement. Each of these is treated in this chapter.

Strategy Relevance of Quality,
Perceived Quality, and Price

Product quantity and quality are the primary performance measures usually associated with manufacturing. These measures jointly determine product cost and also the price that can be charged. However, this simplistic notion is much less clear and more complex in practice.

Delivered quality, for instance, is a term that seems to be unambiguous. However, the quality of a product will be influenced by everything from the personal values of the designer or division manager to the characteristics of available raw materials and the skills of production employees. Further, the process of maintaining a common quality standard among all the components of a finished product may be extremely difficult.

As in any human endeavor, perceptions may be different from reality. Thus, *perceived quality* is another important quality measure. The television industry has been described as one in which it has frequently been difficult to synchronize product quality, customers' quality perceptions, and price. Frustrated executives responsible for the Admiral product line lamented that their facilities could only build "Cadillac quality" appliances, even though consumers never visualized the televisions to be of such quality. Similar concerns were expressed by Westinghouse managers prior to the sale of that firm's home appliance business. In effect, real quality was apparently out of balance with perceived quality, so establishing an appropriate price was impractical.

At the other extreme, when the Head Ski Company introduced its laminated metal skis many years ago, it found the market very willing to pay premium prices for the status of perceived quality; the superior cost effectiveness (real quality) was discovered only secondarily through customers' experiences with using the product.

Thus, the match between quality, perceived quality, cost, and price is a delicate one. In some situations, such as the home appliance market, high quality, if unmatched by perceived quality, can lead to an inability to achieve prices that are commensurate with cost. In other markets, perceived quality, such as that associated with innovative skis, may make high prices practical, whether or not they are warranted by the product's initial cost.

Closely related to the matter of perceived quality is that of innovation in production technologies. Because changes in manufacturing processes can have effects on both quality and price, it is important for the strategic analyst to assess the rate of possible introduction of new technology and the resulting consequences for a firm's competitive positions. New processes that reduce the production costs of commodity chemicals, for example, may offer significant profit potential for the innovator if there is an industry-wide capacity shortage.

The experiences of the Timex Corporation in introducing a new automated production technology into the tradition-bound "Swiss made" watch industry proved to be a challenge on many fronts. Changing product design and introducing automation procedures were much simpler tasks than locating a distribution system (jewelers did not want to handle cheap watches that they could not repair) and convincing the public that inexpensive watches were both reliable and socially acceptable.[2] In short, Timex found that transferring automated mass production technology from the munitions industry to consumer products was much easier than stimulating compatible changes in the marketing dimensions of the industry—and the former was of significantly less value than it would have been if the latter had been easier.

Comparative Cost Analyses

Because competitors seldom build plants at the same time, of the same size, and with the same technology, there is almost certain to be some difference in the manufacturing cost structures of various competitors. An assessment of the probable fixed and variable costs for two firms will provide a basis for estimating the breakeven points and profitability rates at various sales levels. In Exhibit 6-1, we can begin to anticipate the competitive behaviors of Companies A and B as they may reflect their relative cost structures.

Although both plants are of comparable size, Company B's facility is newer and contains more automated equipment. Hence, it has a higher fixed cost and relatively lower variable costs. Coincidentally, however, both have identical breakeven points at about 4,000 units per year.

In this situation, Company B is apt to become the more aggressive competitor, because it has both more to gain and more to lose by shifts in sales level. This can be seen by noting in Exhibit 6-1 that

EXHIBIT 6-1

Comparative Cost Structures of
Two Businesses

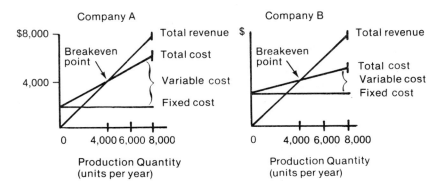

Company A will earn about an extra $1,000 if sales increase from 6,000 to 8,000 units, but Company B will earn an extra $1,500 from the same sales increase. In the same way, a 12½ percent price reduction by B to preserve full capacity will cost it only one-third of its profits, but the same action or response by A would eliminate one-half of its profits.

While the strategic advantages might seem destined to accrue to B in such a case, this is not necessarily the case. Because of A's greater variable cost, it has more opportunity to utilize flexibility for innovation or cost reduction through operating efficiency. In fact, A may partially redefine the market through improved service and custom designed products after B has committed itself to standardized products from its automated production facilities.

Experience Curve Analysis

The potential impact of experience on manufacturing cost differentials, and hence on strategy, is reflected in the concept of the experience curve. The idea is a generalization of the learning curve that has been in use in production for many years.[3]

The experience curve is based on both the learning phenomenon that says that tasks will be done more efficiently as experience is gained at doing them and the empirical observation that firms with the greatest experience tend to be the most profitable.[4] The concept argues that costs of a conversion activity decline at a fixed rate with each doubling of cumulative experience. As suggested in Exhibit 6-2, the firm that can capture a substantial share of a new market early in its development will be in a strong position to stay ahead in operating cost reductions.

EXHIBIT 6-2

Experience Curve Cost Effects

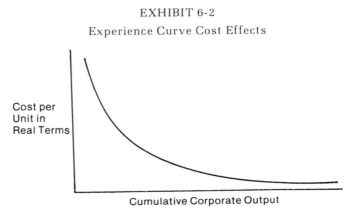

Cost per Unit in Real Terms

Cumulative Corporate Output

Rationale for the Experience Curve

The experience curve reflects economies of scale as well as other phenomena. Economies of scale are those increased efficiencies that are related to size; for instance, a plant with double the capacity of another can usually be built and operated at less than double the cost, thus lowering the unit cost of both capital and operations.

In addition to scale factors, the experience curve reflects the result of the old adage "practice makes perfect." In other words, with greater experience come greater dexterity, cleverness, and skill, which, in turn, can increase efficiency and lower the unit cost.

However, in addition to this learning effect, experience advantages also come through methods improvements, improved organization through greater specialization of tasks or improvements in the mix of resources used in production, and improvements in processes and products that make them simpler and less costly.

Thus, a variety of phenomena can contribute to the experience curve effect. Not all need to operate in any one situation, and indeed some factors may exist while others are absent. Nonetheless, the experience curve has been widely observed in businesses with such diverse products as steam turbine generators, broiler chickens, air conditioners, telephone service, and electric razors. It is widely accepted as a valid phenomenon and a useful basis for strategy development.

Strategic Implications of the Experience Curve

The strategic implications of the experience curve are that, all other things being equal, the firm with the greatest experience can price its product so as to force competitors to suffer low margins or losses. This is because the experienced firm enjoys a cost advantage.

It also has strategic implications for combatting new entrants into a business, since the experienced firm can always price low, perhaps below the new entrant's potential cost, thus forcing the entrant to suffer losses. Although new entrants to a business do generally expect some losses, the experienced firm that practices this strategy can continue to lower its price as its unit costs decline, thus always placing the new entrant in the position of selling at a disadvantageous, and perhaps money-losing, price. A firm following such a strategy can thereby permanently enjoy price advantages that are intolerable in the long run to a new entrant into the market. The knowledge that this is the case may itself be enough to discourage entrants.

The implicit normative conclusion often inferred from experience curve analyses is that a firm should vigorously pursue the largest share

77

of market in order to continuously maintain an advantageous cost position.[5] Such inferences standing alone, however, overlook some critical dimensions of strategy. First, enthusiasm for low-cost production implies that consumer concern for price dominates any interest in such other aspects as product design, innovation, and image.

Support for large-scale production assumes that rivals in an industry will face the limited transferability of cumulative experience from one area of a corporation to another.[6] Also, as many engineers realize, traditional economies of scale often disappear when new production processes are introduced in the form of packaged plants.[7] As part of a wider study of industry structure variables, Michael Porter summarizes his concern with experience curves as follows:

> *Cumulative* experience is only important in and of itself if it is separate from economies of scale, and if the requirement to gain it cannot be avoided by established firms or new entrants.[8]

Most studies regarding experience curves have concerned experience within an industry segment. However, diversified firms that are interested in exploiting cumulative skills in manufacturing or marketing across industries have a potentially valuable asset to manage. In fact, Richard Rumelt's research has revealed relatively high profits in firms that have been able to link their "core skills" to related market segments.[9] It is thus probably not surprising that Texas Instruments was willing to delay its entry into the home computer market until after several other firms had developed initial market positions.[10] The company believed it would be able to transfer accumulated experience in the manufacture of related consumer electronics to the home computer product lines and thus assure low production costs from the outset.

Although most experience curve studies thus far have dealt with manufacturing environments, there is reason to believe that firms in the traditional service sectors will be stimulated to become increasingly cost conscious as a result of Federal Trade Commission actions against architects, accountants, attorneys, engineers, and consultants. When linked with computerized data bases and automated word processing systems, the knowledge of specialists in certain service industries may be distributable at a substantially lower cost than has traditionally been the case. The analyst who is attempting to evaluate a firm's experiences in relationship to those of competitors will thus do well to watch carefully for opportunities or threats associated with potentially unique experiential positions.

Minimum Efficient Scale Facilities

Rather closely related to the idea of experience curves is that of minimum efficient scale (MES) facilities. Because many managers have been taught to think in terms of continuously declining average cost curves, there is often a temptation in the manufacturing field to think that "bigger is better," that one large plant is automatically better than several smaller plants. However, because delivery time and cost of both raw materials and finished goods are sometimes so critical, it is often more desirable from a competitive point of view to operate MES plants in several different geographic locations.

The *rising average cost curve* phenomenon is illustrated in Exhibit 6-3. In this case, the manufacturing cost declines until the added costs of administrative complexity push the curve up at the 20,000 unit per year level. However, because the distribution costs begin to rise at the 10,000 unit level, the total delivered average cost per unit is minimized at about the 15,000 unit per year level.

Thus, the 15,000 unit level is the MES that might provide the basis for a facility location policy in which a number of MES-size facilities are located at various points around the nation or world. The concept of MES facilities partially explains the competitive advantages gained through multiple locations of organizations as diverse as soft drink bottling companies, public accounting firms, and chains of

EXHIBIT 6-3

Minimum Efficient Scale Facility Planning

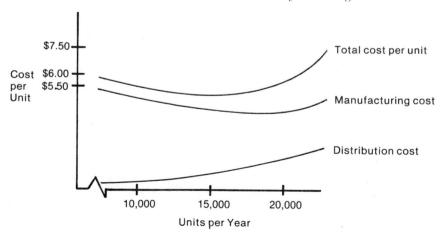

79

nursing homes. Further, it provides the strategist with a direct analytical link to marketing variables that affect costs and customer price sensitivity.[11]

Capacity Utilization Analyses for Strategy

Another issue that is often important in assessing an SBU's strategic posture is that of capacity utilization within an industry. If capacity usage rates are low, it may be very difficult to gain useful cost advantage through modernization of equipment. On the other hand, if usage rates are relatively high, a well-timed modernization or plant expansion decision may provide an opportunity to gain a manufacturing cost advantage that can be translated into an expanded market share.

Beyond the need to choose an appropriate level of automation or labor intensity for a new facility is the problem of selecting appropriate increments of capacity, particularly in expanding markets. The issue is particularly laden with uncertainty early in a product's life cycle, because estimates of long-term demand and final technical characteristics are apt to vary widely. Hence, the pattern of investment is likely to have important implications for long-term profitability.

Perhaps the best way to illustrate the capacity expansion situation in a growing market is through a hypothetical scenario such as that illustrated in Exhibit 6-4.

Through a variety of technical efforts, X Corporation developed and introduced Alpha Product. Because of production difficulties and warranty expenses, no profits were realized until time t_1. As profits became visible after t_1, Y Corporation prepared to enter the market and announced a large construction and market introduction project prior to t_2. X Corporation was concerned about possible excess industry capacity, so it decided to "wait until the next plant is needed." Unfortunately for both X and Y, the Z Corporation had low profits and excess cash, so it decided to enter the market prior to t_3 and accept returns of 15 percent, a rate lower than either X or Y was willing to accept on a new project. Because there were no effective barriers to entry and the original entrants were hesitant about investing, a potential rival with solid assets and low opportunity costs was able to further "carve up" the market. X Corporation's initial monopoly position was rapidly eroded because of its uncertainty and hesitancy, and Y Corporation was unwilling to jump ahead with a second plant, probably because of potential short-term profit declines. This step could have allowed it to dominate two-thirds of the market as it

EXHIBIT 6-4

Returns to Investment in a Growing Market:
An Illustration of Alpha Product

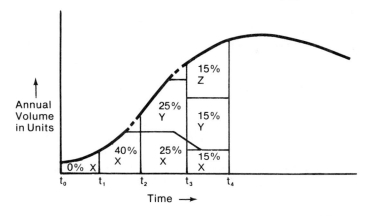

Note: % refers to expected internal rates of return (IRR) at the time
new increments are added.

entered the maturity phase. As a result of this simple scenario, both X
and Y lost a good market position when either might well have
dominated the market.

Obviously, any analysis of the probable actual outcome in a capacity expansion "game" such as this must be accompanied by a detailed
review of such marketing factors as forecasted demand and price
elasticity.[12] One firm that has a reputation for coordinating its multi-
faceted manufacturing decisions with marketing issues very effectively is the Design and Manufacturing Company.[13] Coordinating
aggressive investment in new equipment with plant expansion has
permitted it to retain a low-cost domestic position, and has even given
rise to speculation that D&M might be able to export to Japan in the
1980s.[14]

Materials Management Considerations

In a market-oriented economy operating within an international
atmosphere of free trade, it is easy for managers and analysts to be
lulled into forgetting the critical role played by raw materials. In
order to compensate for past carelessness in this area, many companies are seeking to give explicit recognition to materials security, price,
and flows that extend from overseas sources through transportation
systems and manufacturing processes to final waste disposal. The

81

issue is perceived as being so critical that a senior executive of General Electric, a firm that prides itself in the sophistication of its strategic planning system, has described the new "international integration and resource planning" as "the leading edge of strategic planning."[15]

Although many firms have directed increased attention toward the strategic position of their raw materials sources merely as a result of recent discontinuities in availability or price,[16] other firms have begun to modify the strategic management of their entire materials flow because of its significance in terms of corporate investment.[17]

In firms where the costs of carrying inventory—from raw material through finished goods—constitute a major expense and investment, the idea of integrating all of these functions under a materials manager has begun to gain appeal. In firms where materials constitute a substantial portion of the finished goods investment, the centralization of control over materials—from initial purchase through final product delivery—may be the surest way to reduce investment and ensure continuous flows. *Material requirements planning* (MRP) systems, for example, are designed to link purchasing, inventory, production scheduling, and warehousing activities to ensure timely deliveries without excessive investment.[18]

Strategies that are pursuing cost reduction efforts guided by an MRP system must be carefully synchronized with other functional areas of the SBU if the system is to be effective. For example, the market penetration objectives of various business lines must be carefully coordinated with the MRP system, or the production capacity will not be sufficiently responsive to aggressive marketing thrusts. Further, the information system must permit the entry and retrieval of data on a timely basis at key locations if an MRP system is to be used efficiently for decision-making purposes. When production systems are modified or products redesigned, an MRP system should focus on steps to reduce buffer-stocks, standardize parts across product lines, and otherwise reduce aggregate investment in materials, while simultaneously increasing bargaining power with suppliers for price concessions and with customers for convenient delivery of goods.

When materials are rising in cost and conversion costs are declining, the strategist at the SBU level must pay particular attention to the economics of materials management, or a very critical segment of his or her cost structure may place the firm at a serious disadvantage when generous margins from a significant innovation decline as a result of price competition at a later stage in the product life cycle.

82

Summary

Manufacturing may have been the missing link in corporate strategy a decade ago. It has, however, come to the forefront in the years of shortages and inflation that we have experienced since the early 1970s.

Manufacturing strategy is intrinsically related to quality, perceived quality, and price and to the tradeoffs that must be made among them. The assessment of a business unit's manufacturing position, and therefore its manufacturing policy options, can be made through analyses of comparative costs. Experience curve analysis can amplify this basic assessment to incorporate the potentially significant impacts of organizational learning.

Other strategic assessments in the area of manufacturing can contribute significantly to the manager's understanding of comparative advantage. Minimum efficient scale facilities concepts may modify the thinking that is motivated by comparative cost and experience curve analyses. So too may an assessment of the comparative situations in the industry with respect to capacity utilization. Finally, the strategy for managing materials has become more important in the recent periods of scarcity than ever before. In each of these areas, the operations manager's contribution to the strategic planning effort is being increased, as many firms focus more attention on corporate productivity.[19]

Some of these assessments indicate a search for opportunities such as cost advantages. Others, such as minimum efficient scale plants, tend to reflect possible constraints on the organization. It is only after all have been assessed and integrated that the firm can develop a clear statement of its comparative manufacturing position. Once this has been done, the groundwork for possible strategic change in manufacturing has been established.

Notes

1. Wickham Skinner, "Manufacturing: The Missing Link in Strategy," *Harvard Business Review*, May-June, 1969, pp. 136–145; and S. C. Wheelwright, "Reflecting Corporate Strategy in Manufacturing Decisions," *Business Horizons*, vol. 21, February, 1978, pp. 57–66.

2. See "Timex Corporation" case, Intercollegiate Case Clearing House #6-373-080.

3. W. B. Hirschmann, "Profit from the Learning Curve," *Harvard Business Review*, January-February, 1964, pp. 125–139.

4. R. D. Buzzell, B. T. Gale, and R. G. M. Sultan, "Market Share—A Key to Profitability," *Harvard Business Review*, January-February, 1975, pp. 97–106.

5. For instance, see "Emerson Electric's Rise as a Low-cost Producer," *Business Week*, November 1, 1976, p. 47.

6. For a more complete discussion of these issues, see W. J. Abernathy and K. Wayne, "Limits of the Learning Curve," *Harvard Business Review*, September-October, 1974, pp. 109–119.

7. An interesting example appeared in the form of cogeneration power plants in New York City. See Tom Alexander, "The Little Engine That Scares Con Ed," *Fortune*, December 31, 1978, pp. 80–84.

8. Michael E. Porter, "Note on the Structural Analysis of Industries," ICCH #9-376-054, 1975. Also see his *Competitive Strategy: Techniques for Analyzing Industries and Competitors* (New York: The Free Press, 1980).

9. Richard P. Rumelt, "Diversity and Profitability," Working Paper #MGL-51, U.C.L.A., 1977; and Kathryn R. Harrigan, "Strategy Formulation in Declining Industries," *The Academy of Management Review*, October, 1980, pp. 599–604.

10. "Texas Instruments Pounces on Market in Home Computers," *Wall Street Journal*, June 1, 1979, p. 8. Subsequent difficulties were documented in "When Marketing Failed at Texas Instruments," *Business Week*, June 22, 1981, pp. 91–94.

11. For research regarding the strategic implications of MES facilities in the home appliance industry, see Michael S. Hunt, "Competition in the Major Home Appliance Industry, 1960–1970" (Boston: Harvard Business School, unpublished doctoral dissertation, 1972).

12. For an example of systematic research on these problems, see Ram C. Rao, and David Rutenberg, "Preempting an Alert Rival: Strategic Timing of the First Plant by Analysis of Sophisticated Rivalry," *The Bell Journal of Economics*, Autumn, 1979, pp. 412–428.

13. The strategy of the company is well documented in the "Design and Manufacturing Company" case in C. R. Christensen, K. Andrews, and J. L. Bower, *Business Policy: Text and Cases*, 4th edition (Homewood, Illinois: R. D. Irwin, 1978), pp. 416–424. A recent recap of Samuel Regenstrief's financial success is contained in Arthur M. Louis, "In Search of the Elusive Big Rich," *Fortune*, February 12, 1979, p. 92.

14. For a broader review of international plant location considerations, see Robert B. Stobaugh, "Where in the World Should We Put That Plant?" *Harvard Business Review*, January-February, 1969, pp. 129–136.

15. "The New Planning," *Business Week*, December 18, 1978, p. 68.

16. A. A. Meitz and Breaux B. Castleman, "How to Cope with Supply Shortages," *Harvard Business Review*, January-February, 1975, pp. 91–96.

17. Jeffrey G. Miller and Peter Gilmour, "Materials Managers: Who Needs Them?" *Harvard Business Review*, July-August, 1979, pp. 143–153.

18. Robert W. Hall and T. E. Vollmann, "Planning Your Material Requirements," *Harvard Business Review*, September-October, 1978, pp. 105–112.

19. Robert Lubar, "Rediscovering the Factory," *Fortune*, July 13, 1981, pp. 52–56, 60, 64.

CHAPTER 7

Research and Development and Human Resources Aspects of Strategy Analysis

THIS CHAPTER explores the internal analyses aspect of Exhibits 2–3 and 2–5 (for the integrated and diversified firm respectively) in the domains of research and development (R&D) and human resources management (HRM). As in Chapters 3–6, the perspective taken is generally that of the business unit.

This chapter treats research and development strategy in terms of product R&D, process R&D, the timing dimension of R&D, and the relationships of R&D to overall business strategy. Human resources strategy is dealt with in terms of labor market–based planning and the need to develop motivational and incentive systems.

R&D Components of Strategy

The position a firm chooses to take with respect to the management of its technological resources must be closely linked to other variables if revenues are to be stimulated and investment is to be controlled. The firm that permits its "creeping capability" in the research laboratory to lead it casually into new markets or processes may discover belatedly that it does not have the marketing system or skilled personnel to make the innovation a commercial success. One respected firm, for example, permitted two trusted chemists to spend more than $1 million over a five-year period trying to develop a new golf ball even though the firm did not have a marketing system that would have permitted the effective sale of such a new product if it had materialized.[1]

Product R&D

The first important issue that one must try to resolve in product R&D is the question of whether the work is being undertaken for offensive or defensive purposes. Offensive projects are those pursued with the intent of replacing an existing product, attacking a competitor's product, or satisfying a new customer need. In any event, offensive projects are designed to reach the marketplace as soon as they are technically and economically feasible, without particular concern about cannibalizing existing products.

Defensive projects, on the other hand, are those intended to supplement or supplant existing products if they should be subjected to serious competitive pressures. The assumption in such situations is that premature introduction of a new technology will unnecessarily jeopardize profits of an existing product line. Further, firms typically have an incentive to stimulate competitors to focus on an "easy product target" in the hopes that the firms can counterattack with the next generation of technology and thereby increase the competitors' expenses and reduce their flexibility.[2]

Process R&D

The task of analyzing a firm's strategic posture in the area of technology does not end with concerns over new product introductions. Securing the appropriate balance in R&D effort between process-oriented work designed to allow existing activities to be performed more efficiently and product-oriented work aimed at serving customers' needs more effectively is the fundamental allocation difficulty.[3] In order for changes in manufacturing processes to be introduced effectively, there must be recognition of the need for coordination with marketing plans regarding demand and price, with the human resources area for training and/or relocation requirements, and with the financial planning function for estimates of cash availability and profit impacts. Inability to maintain essential confidentiality while at the same time orchestrating a sequence of resource shifts can seriously undermine the strategic effectiveness of R&D investment in new process developments. In spite of these managerial complexities, many firms have sustained a competitive advantage in technical innovation for years.[4]

86

Relating R&D Projects
to Overall Strategy

There is a clear need to ensure that R&D projects, as well as all other organizational activities, are directly related to the firm's strategic posture. If this is not done, the firm may well become involved in peripheral activities that have the effect of dissipating its resources. While this would be unusual in a marketing area, where the focus is on generating revenue, it is not all that unusual in the R&D area, where more complex goals and motives, such as the satisfaction of the technical interests of individual researchers and scientists, may come into play.

For instance, in an audit of the existing and planned programs in the central research laboratory of a major diversified firm, one of the authors found:

1. Programs and projects that could not be associated with any business or corporate objective or strategy.
2. Programs and projects that apparently fell outside the stated mission of the corporation or the charter of the laboratory.
3. Projects with funding levels that could not reasonably be justified in terms of the expected benefits to be produced.[5]

An R&D evaluation framework The general framework for evaluating how well R&D projects and programs fit into the overall strategic posture of the business is shown in Exhibit 7-1. It shows a wide variety of potential projects and programs being filtered through the application of strategic criteria based on the higher-level choices that have previously been made—the organization's mission, objectives, and strategy. The output of this filtering process is a set of rank-ordered project and program opportunities that can serve as a basis for the allocation of resources. (The rank-ordering process is shown in Exhibit 7-2.)

Other important criteria must come into play in implementing this evaluation process. Together these generic criteria make up a good specification of the organization's mission, objectives, and strategy. However, they must be specifically addressed if programs and projects are to truly reflect corporate strategy. The criteria:

1. Does the opportunity take advantage of a *strength* that the company possesses?
2. Correspondingly, does it avoid a dependence on a *weakness* of the firm?

87

EXHIBIT 7-1

Strategic Evaluation of Programs and
Projects

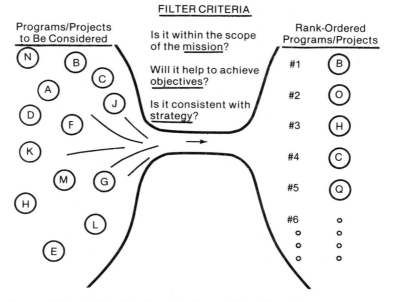

FILTER CRITERIA

Programs/Projects to Be Considered

Is it within the scope of the <u>mission</u>?

Will it help to achieve <u>objectives</u>?

Is it consistent with <u>strategy</u>?

Rank-Ordered Programs/Projects

#1 B
#2 O
#3 H
#4 C
#5 Q
#6

Source: William R. King, "Implementing Strategic Plans Through Strategic Program Evaluation," *OMEGA: The International Journal of Management Science*, vol. 8, no. 2, 1980, pp. 173-181. With permission of the publisher.

3. Does it offer the opportunity to attain a *comparative advantage* over competitors?
4. Does it contribute to the *internal consistency* of the existing projects and programs?
5. Does it address a *mission-related opportunity* that is presented by the evolving market environment?
6. Is it consistent with established *policy guidelines*?
7. Is the level of *risk* acceptable?

An R&D evaluation process   Exhibit 7-2 shows an analysis that can be conducted to evaluate the linkage between specific projects and programs and the overall strategic posture.

The criteria weights in the second column of the exhibit reflect the relative importance of the criteria and permit the evaluation and illustration of complex project characteristics within a simple framework. A base weight of 20 is used for the major criteria related to mission, objectives, strategy, and goals. Weights of 10 are applied to the generic criteria.

EXHIBIT 7-2

Strategic Program Evaluation—An Example

Program/project evaluation criteria		Criteria weights	Very good (8)	Good (6)	Fair (4)	Poor (2)	Very poor (0)	Expected level score	Weighted score
'Fit' with the mission	Product	10	1.0					8.0	80
	Market	10	1.0					8.0	80
Consistency with objectives	ROI	10	0.2	0.6	0.2			6.0	60
	Dividends	5		0.2	0.6	0.2		4.0	20
	Image	5			0.8	0.2		3.6	18
Consistency with strategy	Stage 1	10					1.0	0	0
	Stage 2	7	1.0					8.0	56
	Stage 3	3					1.0	0	0
Contribution to goals	Goal A	8					1.0	0	0
	Goal B	6	0.8	0.2				7.6	45.6
	Goal C	4		0.8	0.2			5.6	22.4
	Goal D	2					1.0	0	0
Corporate *strength* base		10				0.8	0.2	1.6	16
Corporate *weakness* avoidance		10				0.2	0.8	0.4	4
Comparative advantage level		10	0.7	0.3				7.4	74
Internal consistency level		10	1.0					8.0	80
Mission-related opportunity		10	1.0					8.0	80
Risk level acceptability		10				0.7	0.3	1.4	14
Policy guideline consistency		10			1.0			4.0	40
Total weighted score									690

Source: This exhibit is based on one in William R. King, "Implementing Strategic Plans Through Strategic Program Evaluation," *OMEGA,The International Journal of Management Science,* vol. 8, no. 2, 1980, pp. 173–181. With permission of the publisher.

Within each major category, the 20 points are judgmentally distributed to reflect the relative importance of subelements or some other characteristics of the criterion. For instance, the strategy in Exhibit 7-2 is shown to have three stages, which might reflect the time horizon of the various subelements of an overall strategy. The strategy may be, for example, to first enlarge sales to existing customers and then focus on new customers. In the exhibit, the substrategies and the four subgoals are weighted to ensure that earlier stages and goals are treated as more important than later ones. This might implicitly reflect the time value of money in order to avoid complex discounting calculation.

The first criterion in Exhibit 7-2 is the "'fit' with the mission." The proposal is evaluated to be consistent with both the product and market elements of the mission and is thereby rated very good, as shown by the 1.0 entries in the upper left.

In terms of "consistency with objectives," the proposal is rated to have a 20 percent chance of being "very good" in contributing to the ROI element of the objectives, a 60 percent chance of being "good," and a 20 percent chance of being only "fair," as indicated by the likelihoods entered into the third row of the table. The proposed project is rated more poorly with respect to the Dividends and Image elements.

The proposal is also evaluated in terms of its expected contribution to each of the three stages of the strategy. In this case, the proposed project is believed to be one that would contribute principally to stage 2 of the strategy. (Note that only certain assessments are made in this case, since the stages are mutually exclusive and exhaustive, but this would not always be true.)

The proposal is similarly evaluated with respect to the other criteria.

The overall evaluation is obtained as a weighted score that represents the sum of products of the likelihoods (probabilities) and the 8, 6, 4, 2, and 0 arbitrary level weights that are displayed at the top of the exhibit. For instance, the "consistency with objectives–ROI" expected level weight is calculated as

$$0.2(8) + 0.6(6) + 0.2(4) = 6.0$$

This is then multiplied by the criterion weight of 10 to obtain a weighted score of 60. The weighted scores are then summed to obtain an overall evaluation of 690.

Of course, this number in isolation is meaningless. However, when various programs and projects are evaluated in terms of the same criteria, their overall scores provide a reasonable basis for developing the ranking shown on the right side of Exhibit 7-1. Such a ranking can be the basis for strategic resource allocation, since the top-ranked program is presumed to be the most worthy, the second-ranked the next most worthy, and so on.

R&D Timing

When the strategic objectives of a project have been defined and the expected scope of the proposal has been articulated, it becomes important to focus on the timing and sequencing of the development efforts. Often projects that can be undertaken simultaneously in the research laboratory cannot be implemented simultaneously because of personnel or capital constraints that will occur later in the development cycle. Even firms the size of General Electric can be forced to make undesirable choices if markets grow too fast or become overly attractive to new competitors.[6] In spite of the theoretical availability of capital from external sources to fund "good projects," most firms are extremely reluctant to secure large amounts of outside capital for multiple major investments. Their caution may, in fact, reflect a justifiable concern about the firm's ability to monitor and control many arenas of newness simultaneously.

Although the cash flow and internal rate of return (IRR) effects of R&D projects and the related development plans may be adequately reflected in a project proposal, it is often difficult to predict the income or "earnings per share" effects without summarizing the individual projects in a format such as Exhibit 7-3.

Because, within a certain range, many firms view R&D as a discretionary or managed expense, it is crucial that the senior officers be in a position to observe and monitor the R&D expense levels for various business units and areas of technology at the same time that they are analyzing other dimensions of subunit performance.

Unless subunit performance is measured over time periods commensurate with strategic objectives and in multiple dimensions, some managers will always be tempted to spend R&D funds to try to "save," with a "great breakthrough," a business unit already slated for harvesting or divestiture. Alternatively, some units targeted for market share growth may overemphasize marketing efforts to the detriment of the technical lead essential for the sustenance of a major market share.[7]

Because it is often very interesting and challenging for technical innovators to continually improve a product, the analyst evaluating comparative product positions must be critical in assessing when new product improvements stop adding value and simply add cost. The real problem, of course, is in knowing at any given time how many

EXHIBIT 7-3

R&D Cash Flow Monitoring Framework

	Investment to Year T (incomplete projects)	T	T + 1	T + 2	T + 3	Beyond
A. Government sector						
1. Electronics market						
a. Delta project	$					
b. Gamma project	$	$	$	$	(manufacture or divest)	
2. Aircraft market						
a.		$	(market or sell)			
b.		0	$			
3. Health services						
Subtotal	$	$	$	$	$	$
B. Industrial sector						
1. Control systems				(make or shift to new technology)		
a.		$	$			
b.		0	$	$	$	
c.						
2. Truck parts						
a.						
b.						
Subtotal	$	$	$	$	$	$
C. Consumer sector						
1. Appliances						
a.						
b.						
c.						
2. Hand tools						
a.						
3. Toys						
a.						
Subtotal	$	$	$	$	$	$
Total	$	$	$	$	$	$

customers want a stable technology at a lower cost and how many want state-of-the-art innovation. These difficulties are well illustrated by the case of Aerosol Techniques, Inc. (ATI) during the aerosol's period of initial product maturity. Many private-label hairspray producers wanted an aerosol mechanism that was reliable and cheap, but many ATI executives wanted to continue experimenting with things that "were new and exciting." It was not until several bankruptcies and a couple major new entries into the industry had occurred that ATI seemed to really recognize the implications of the "new game." A similar problem is almost constantly present in the industrial systems business, and those firms that have developed systematic criteria for deciding when to transfer new products to standardized production environments and when to return the technical innovators to the R&D labs have been able to increase profitability faster than those that have continued extensive custom engineering on each new job. The need to carefully plan and control strategic investments in advanced technical projects will never be greater than in the decade ahead.[8]

Human Resources
Aspects of Strategy Analysis

The assessment of human resources skills often receives less attention than almost any other set of factors in strategic planning systems. Unfortunately, many analysts view the labor force as being almost infinitely available, mobile, and malleable, when in fact the number of rigidities or constraints is substantial and is generally increasing.[9]

The Labor Market

One can begin a strategic analysis by quantifying labor costs among competitors to see which may have a distinct advantage or burden. Many domestic firms have been announcing decisions to "move south" or "into a smaller community" in order to reduce labor costs. Although such decisions may seem to be justifiable, some firms have discovered shortages of specialized skills in small communities, so expansion or production changes have been costly to implement. Others have found that deregulation has meant the loss of scheduled airline service to their small-town plants, so marketing expenses have risen dramatically because of the need for added sales personnel or private airplane service.

The competition for skilled employees within a small market is apt to be more direct and more intense than in a larger community. The problem is poignantly illustrated in the Hedblom case[10] in which the company has to consider the sale of its old textile plant. The worst possible option would be to sell it to the highest logical bidder— another textile firm—because most of the workers who are being transported to the "new efficient plant" would prefer to work in the older plant closer to their homes.

Anticipating potential new employers in a small local labor market is often a valuable exercise, because a few new employers who can

93

afford to pay premium wages are apt to attract the most talented workers or push up the general wage rate. If one of those new employers happens to be a sister division from a different industry or one of your multiproduct arch-rivals, the secondary consequences of its relocation decision could be genuinely costly to your competitive position. If unionization issues are involved, more complexities unfold.

Unionization differences among competitors is another factor that can influence both hourly wages and production stability. The Frigidaire Division of General Motors, for example, was long recognized by appliance industry analysts to be at a cost disadvantage because its production employees were covered by UAW contracts at about $1.00 per hour above the appliance industry norms. Negotiations suggesting possible divestiture and a variety of other tactics were raised by GM as part of its effort to remain labor cost competitive in the appliance industry.[11] This industry also provides a good example of the shifting bases of competitive interaction across segments, as firms such as Raytheon and Litton enter the high technology arenas and firms with traditional reputations for manufacturing expertise such as Westinghouse, Rockwell, and GM are squeezed out of the price-sensitive segments by White Consolidated and Magic Chef.

In addition to production labor cost comparisons, an analyst must also study the relative abilities and incentives within the administrative, marketing, R&D, and other nonmanufacturing labor groups that may be important in a given industry. Geographic and employer mobility is generally greater among the professional employees, so remaining competitive in a national labor pool is often easier for such employees than for the less mobile production work force. This issue was highlighted in the securities industry when Merrill Lynch acquired the assets of White Weld,[12] only to find the most valuable assets, the brokers, resigning in large numbers and taking their account contacts with them to competitors' offices. The fact that a firm "can't take title to its human assets" was recognized too late, and Merrill Lynch's competitors in many metropolitan markets ended up being relatively *stronger*, rather than weaker, as a result of Merrill Lynch's effort to strengthen its position!

In a contrasting situation, Boeing Company "borrowed" almost one thousand engineers from prospective subcontractors for two major airframe developments it was pursuing simultaneously.[13] Rather than delay development of a strategic project or risk massive layoffs at a later time, Boeing gained flexibility without unnecessarily burdensome fixed costs.

Incentives and Administrative Systems

In addition to planning for requisite numbers of employees across various skill classes and assessing the availability and cost of personnel in the external labor market, the strategist must also consider the implications of evolving employee expectations for the general structure of incentives and the work environment. Some motivational systems that have been used for decades may lose their effectiveness or may need to be extended to more job categories as dual-career families face higher marginal income tax rates and seek greater schedule flexibility.[14] In order to respond to such diverse motivations, the Sony Corporation, as an example, has broadened the scope of its operations in order to provide challenging alternative career paths for those employees who want to leave electronics but stay with Sony Corporation.[15]

Closely allied to the need to evaluate the differential effects of changing incentives on employees is the need to study the competitive significance of what might be termed *administrative efficiency and flexibility*. Small, entrepreneurially oriented firms are often viewed as having advantages over large corporations in areas where adaptability to local customs, codes, and such is deemed to be critical. On the other hand, such small firms are thought to be hampered by lack of access to sophisticated accounting, inventory control, and related computer systems. However, the rapidly declining costs of data transmission and processing are simultaneously making the small local firms more sophisticated and timely, and their giant competitors more flexible and adaptable. In short, administrative technology is rapidly changing some important bases for competition within industries as diverse as tax return preparation services, grocery stores,[16] and legal services.

While advancing technology aids and stimulates flexibility and adaptability, strategists may find that they are being slowed and constrained by societal changes. Employment security may limit broad changes, but flex-time schedules and educational programs can be seen as facilitating adaptation to some changing needs. Perhaps the most important admonition for the analyst to remember in assessing relative strategic positions in the human resources area is that a head count may be an extremely deceptive indicator. We may, in fact, by well served by the advice attributed to Aristotle and dating from about 2500 years ago:

And even if we reckon greatness by numbers, we ought *not* to

95

include everybody, for there must always be in cities a multitude of slaves and sojourners and foreigners; but we should include those only who are members of the state, and who form *an essential part* of it.[17] [Emphasis added.]

The taxing strategic problems that arose within a major European consulting firm as it tried to redirect its professional services away from "production line techniques" and toward "international strategic planning" amply demonstrate the inflexibilities associated with decades of specialization and general inattention to changes in contiguous market segments. [18] Under such circumstances, a key function of the strategist is to select a market sector (arena) in which the firm's critical human resources will have a comparative advantage while the organization bears the costs of adaptation (retraining and relocation).

Fortunately, however, James Craft and others have recognized the need for improved planning and information systems for the human resources aspect of strategic planning.[19] Specific systems which recognize the diverse needs of employees and evolving organizational requirements promise to provide increasing assistance to strategists in the years ahead.

The analysis of human resources capabilities poses a special problem for the strategist, because in most organizations the relative quality of the personnel from the board of directors to the production line is both critical and extremely difficult to measure satisfactorily. Further, it is one resource with a relative value that can change significantly as the result of such elusive phenomena as leadership or organizational climate. Finally, the mere act of trying to measure or evaluate this resource may influence its value in either a positive or a negative direction.

Summary

The research and development and human resources strategies of the business unit are dealt with in this chapter. These have often been considered to be of secondary importance to some of the other functional area strategies. However, the increasing need of American business to gain comparative advantage through technology, while existing in an environment of greater human sensitivity and greater demands of employees, has brought these strategic areas into greater prominence.

This chapter concludes the series of four chapters dealing with strategic assessment in specific functional areas in the business unit. In Chapter 8, we return to analysis at the business unit level.

Notes

1. A similar but more serious lack of strategic control can be seen in the experiences surrounding FIREGUARD in the "Industrial Products" case in C. R. Christensen, K. Andrews, and J. L. Bower, *Business Policy: Text & Cases*, 4th ed. (Homewood, Illinois: R. D. Irwin, 1978).

2. H. I. Ansoff and John M. Stewart, "Strategies for Technology-based Business," *Harvard Business Review*, November-December, 1967, pp. 71–83.

3. For a recent study seeking to evaluate these tradeoffs in the automobile industry, see William J. Abernathy, *The Productivity Dilemma* (Baltimore: The Johns Hopkins University Press, 1978).

4. For a description of the way in which one disguised firm overcame its excessive preoccupation with financial controls to the detriment of R&D, see Frederick W. Gluck, Richard N. Foster, and John L. Forbis, "Cure for Strategic Malnutrition," *Harvard Business Review*, November-December, 1976, pp. 154–165.

5. William R. King, "Implementing Strategic Plans Through Strategic Program Evaluation," *OMEGA, The International Journal of Management Science*, vol. 8, no. 2, 1980, pp. 173–181.

6. See further analysis of the tradeoffs for GE among computers, jet engines, and nuclear power plants in William E. Fruhan, Jr., "Pyrrhic Victories in the Fight for Market Share," *Harvard Business Review*, September-October, 1972, pp. 100–107.

7. For additional discussion of frameworks for evaluating major new technical proposals, see George R. White and M. B. W. Graham, "How to Spot a Technological Winner," *Harvard Business Review*, March-April, 1978, pp. 146–152; and William D. Zarecor, "High Technology Product Planning," *Harvard Business Review*, January-February, 1975, pp. 108–115. For the impact of R&D spending on ROI, see Kurt Christensen, "Product, Market and Company Influences upon Profitability of Business Unit R&D Expenditures," unpublished dissertation, Columbia University, 1977.

8. See J. H. Grant, "Management Implications of Systems-Oriented Strategies Within Selected Industrial Firms: A Developmental Model," unpublished dissertation, Harvard Business School, 1972; "Technologies for the '80s," *Business Week*, July 6, 1981, pp. 48–52, 56.

9. D. Quinn Mills, "Human Resources in the 1980's," *Harvard Business Review*, July-August, 1979, pp. 154–162.

10. "Hedblom (A)," Intercollegiate Case Clearing House #6-369-047.

11. Amanda Bennett, "Evidence Mounts That GM Is Considering a Retreat from the Appliance Business," *Wall Street Journal*, January 22, 1979, p. 3; and "White Consolidated's New Appliance Punch," *Business Week*, May 7, 1979, p. 94.

12. Lee Smith, "The Mauling Merrill Lynch Never Expected," *Fortune*, October 23, 1978, pp. 78–79, 82, 84, 88, 90. A somewhat similar example from the public accounting profession is described in Stanley H. Brow, "Why Lasser Found Touche Ross Taxing," *Fortune*, May 18, 1981, pp. 103–104, 107.

13. "Boeing's Great Engineer Grab," *Newsweek*, July 9, 1979, p. 59.

14. D. Quinn Mills, "Human Resources," *Harvard Business Review*, July-August, 1979, pp. 154–162.

15. "Sony: A Diversification Plan Tuned to the People Factor," *Business Week*, February 9, 1981, pp. 88–90.

16. Paul Ingrassia, "Independent Grocers Outsell the Big Chains by Adapting to Markets," *Wall Street Journal*, November 28, 1978, pp. 1, 22.

17. Aristotle, *Politics*, book VI, The Great Books of the Western World, vol. I (Chicago: Encyclopaedia Britannica, Inc., 1952), p 325.

18. "Raadgvend Bureau Ir. B. W. Berenschot N. V.," case series in C. R. Christensen, K. R. Andrews, and J. L. Bower, *Business Policy: Text and Cases*, 3rd ed. (Homewood, Illinois: R. D. Irwin, 1973), pp. 522–577.

19. James A. Craft, "Human Resources Planning: An Emerging Dimension of Management," *Managing*, no. 3, 1979, pp. 5, 32.

CHAPTER 8

Integrated
Strategic Analyses

CHAPTERS 1 AND 2 presented the overall framework for strategic
planning. Chapter 3 was the first of a series of chapters that elaborated
on the internal analysis aspect of that framework, dealing with overall
preliminary analyses at the business unit level and then with internal
analyses in the finance, marketing, manufacturing, R&D, and human
resources areas.

This chapter again addresses integrated analyses at the business
unit level. The analyses discussed here are generally best undertaken
after analyses have been performed in the various functional areas.
There is no clear conceptual distinction between the analyses of this
chapter and those of Chapter 3, except a sequential one—those described in Chapter 3 are best thought of as preliminary, while those
presented in this chapter are summary.

The two principal varieties of strategic analysis discussed here are
PIMS analyses and integrated analyses. Analyses based on PIMS are
specific tools that can be used to preliminarily assess the overall performance of a business unit. The integrated analyses are illustrative of
those that may be executed in moving from functional-based internal
analyses to comprehensive business unit strategic analysis.

PIMS Analyses

PIMS provides one of the most interesting and potentially useful
overall analyses of a business unit's strategic posture. PIMS (Profitability Impact of Marketing Strategy) refers broadly to a large data
base containing measures of strategic variables from more than 1000
business units and a set of cross-sectional regression models used to
study the impacts of different factors on the economic performance

99

of a business unit. The continuing project is designed to provide managers with improved insights into the combinations of strategic posture, market environment, and competitive levels that are most apt to yield desired performance levels. This is done by providing data that are statistically compared with similar data provided by other business units.

For PIMS purposes, a business unit is defined as an operating unit that sells a distinct set of products or services to an identifiable group of customers in competition with a well-defined set of competitors. Participating firms provide more than 100 data items on prescribed forms to the Strategic Planning Institute. These items describe the business, products, customers, relationships with other businesses in the same company, operating results, balance sheet information, competitors, and assumptions about future sales, costs, and prices.

PIMS is based on the idea that when comparable data on many business units are compared, despite the intrinsic differences among the businesses, certain strategic characteristics that relate to performance will be identifiable.

Using PIMS

There are two general ways in which PIMS may prove useful in the strategic assessment of a business unit—through its general findings and through comparison of one business unit's data with that of other business units to suggest areas that might be productive for strategic change.

General PIMS findings The PIMS data base is so rich that it provides a potentially powerful base for research into the nature and "cause" of business unit profitability. Multivariate regression equations are used to estimate the relationship between various business unit characteristics and two performance variables—ROI and cash flow.

These, as well as various simple cross-tabulations, are used to infer the relationships that may exist between various factors. For instance, one well-known result is that ROI is closely related to market share—businesses with high market share tend to enjoy high levels of ROI.[1] This may be interpreted to suggest that market share "causes" ROI and that the way to achieve high ROI is through high market share. However, such interpretations may not be warranted, despite the fact that they are often made.

Such results are not conclusive for a variety of technical reasons that need not be pursued here.[2] For our purposes, it is important to note only that while general findings may suggest strategies or ap-

100

proaches that should be considered by a business, such results are neither definitive nor even necessarily valid. The PIMS data base has been useful for academic researchers who are interested in studying specialized strategies consisting of carefully selected combinations of operating factors. Ralph Biggadike's study of new market entry strategies, for example, led to the conclusions that (1) large-scale entries are necessary for success in growth markets and (2) relative market share achievement and capitalized ROI are good evaluation measures for entry strategies.[3] Other research by Carolyn Woo and Arnold Cooper permitted them to isolate certain conditions under which a low market share position would not necessarily lead to the dismal ROI results that are commonly assumed.[4]

Business unit comparisons   A second, and perhaps more important, use for PIMS is based on comparisons of the statistics for one business with those of other businesses in the PIMS data base. For example, the PAR reports indicate the "normal" levels of ROI or cash flow for a business with particular characteristics. Strategy Sensitivity Reports, on the other hand, show the likely results of making assumed strategic changes in a business strategy. Comparisons may also be made with the overall averages for all businesses in the data base. These comparisons may be useful in establishing performance expectations for each business, since such standards should closely reflect the particular situation in which a business must operate.

The business factors that contribute to deviations from "normal" performance may be used to suggest critical strategic factors that might be manipulated by the business. For instance, one business unit used the PIMS analysis to identify a number of factors—product quality, degree of vertical integration, and sales direct to end users— that statistically had a deleterious effect on performance. These were seen as characteristics that were holding the SBU back from achieving its best performance. The business studied ways in which these strategic factors might therefore be manipulated to better effect.

PIMS Strategy Sensitivity Reports predict what might occur if postulated changes were made in the business unit's strategic posture. These predictions should not be used as specific forecasts, but in the "What if?" spirit of developing a better understanding of the relative merits of various strategic changes. They can also be used to explore the time dimension of strategic performance—for instance, by assessing the short-run negative impact on cash flow of improved market share versus its expected long-run positive impact.

Of course, all of these analyses are based on the PIMS models, which are not open to public scrutiny, and on assumptions made by each business unit as its inputs to the PIMS models. These assumptions

101

involve predictions of future costs, prices, and other factors, and are therefore themselves subject to substantial potential error.

Thus, the use of pooled business data can provide an interesting and potentially useful basis for assessing a business unit's performance relative to that of other such units and for suggesting strategic changes that might prove to be beneficial. As long as such assessments are considered merely suggestive, the tool is being properly used. With their many limitations and potential defects, tools such as those from the PIMS project can be readily misused. The potential for harm is great because the elements that are being manipulated are truly strategic ones. The wise strategic analyst will therefore use the tool, but will do so with great reserve and caution.

Other Integrated Strategic Analyses

A wide variety of analyses can be performed after the various functional-based analyses, as demonstrated in Chapters 4–7, have been performed. Here we illustrate some such integrated analyses, as they provide stepping-stones from separate functional analyses to comprehensive strategic business unit assessment.

Assessment of Impact on
Multiple Business Units

When an activity has a direct and significant impact on the performance of many different business units within a firm, the strategic analyst is pushed toward integrated analyses. This is often the case with R&D projects. To illustrate, consider the plots of several different R&D projects for a multiindustry firm in Exhibit 8-1. Because projects W, X, and Z are foreseen as having application in individual divisions, the assignment of costs and benefits is relatively simple. On the other hand, projects U, V, and Y are expected to make conditional contributions to business lines in more than one sector or group within the corporation. Given the elapsed time and the uncertainty regarding technical achievement and competitors' responses, it would be very difficult to assign net present values to the spin-offs from the original pieces of proposed research. Failure to do so, however, might force the delay or termination of a project such as U or Y, which might yield competitive advantages in several market arenas.

Thus, while there is no simple solution to this difficult problem of interdependencies, a planning framework such as Exhibit 8-1 provides the basis for keeping track of projects and ensuring that they are fairly evaluated with respect to both their costs and their potential multidivisional benefits.

102

EXHIBIT 8-1

Research and Development
Integrated Planning Framework

Product-market Position	Performance Dimensions			
	Technical Feasibility	Market Penetration	Return on Investment	Cash Flow
A. Governmental Sector				
1.				U
2.				V
3.		W		
B. Industrial Sector				
1.				V
2.				X
3.				U
4.				Y
C. Consumer Sector				
1.				Y'
2.				U''
3.				Z

←————— Time ————→

Interdependent Analyses of Functions

Many cross-functional analyses are directly suggested by the functional ones. For instance, after the technical boundaries of a proposed R&D project have been tentatively identified, it becomes important that project evaluations be expanded to include equipment, warehousing, working capital, sales force expansion, and related investments that may be required before sales actually materialize. Unfortunately, many sophisticated firms permit incomplete project definitions to be funded through R&D budgets or the capital budgeting process without adequate specification of the full investment required.

In another sphere, Robert Hayes and Steven Wheelwright have proposed a framework for linking some important decisions in the operations area to those in marketing.[5] The strategist who is concerned with the tradeoffs between manufacturing flexibility and cost reduction concepts will find it useful to position a product line on a matrix similar to Exhibit 8-2 and ask the question "In which direction do we want *this* product line to move in the future?" A product line strategy designed to maximize custom design efforts, for example, would lead to a flexible job shop environment, while a high-volume

103

EXHIBIT 8-2

Life Cycles Matrix
for Products and Processes

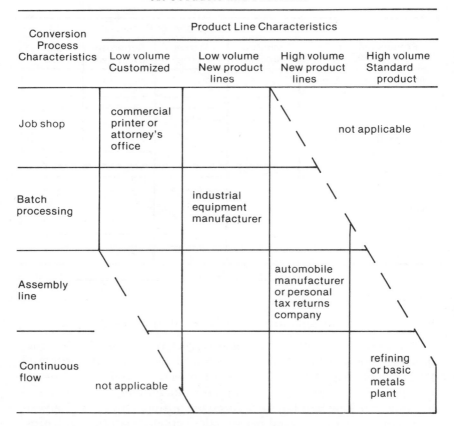

Conversion Process Characteristics	Product Line Characteristics			
	Low volume Customized	Low volume New product lines	High volume New product lines	High volume Standard product
Job shop	commercial printer or attorney's office			not applicable
Batch processing		industrial equipment manufacturer		
Assembly line			automobile manufacturer or personal tax returns company	
Continuous flow	not applicable			refining or basic metals plant

commodity orientation would suggest a specially designed continuous flow facility.

These relationships may seem simple, but numerous firms have made costly mistakes because the marketing people were developing future customers in one direction while the facility planners were designing in the opposite direction. Obviously, if a firm has idle capacity, there should be a strong incentive to pursue a customer segment for whom products can be manufactured efficiently. Looking outward, the firm that senses a competitor designing a flexible

EXHIBIT 8-3

Interdependency Review Chart for Functions within an SBU: Some Illustrative Examples

Complementing Relationships (upper-right triangle) / Detracting Relationships (lower-left triangle)

	Finance	Marketing	R&D	Manufacturing	Human Resources	Materials	External Relations
Finance	///	can reduce accounts receivable	not applicable				executive leadership yields investor confidence
Marketing	cannot support advertising	///	improve warranty experience		sales incentives attract skilled professionals		
R&D	most projects are over budget	late with new products	///				
Manufacturing				///		new sources ease scheduling	
Human Resources					///		
Materials	not applicable	less customer appeal	not applicable	more frequent breakage	often fail OSHA standards	///	
External Relations			engineers dislike our image				///

105

facility may have an opportunity for aggressive price cutting in the standardized segment of the market.

Testing for Internal Consistency

As indicated in Chapter 3, one of the most important characteristics of a business unit strategy is its internal consistency. Once the necessary functional and cross-functional analyses have been performed, a formal and systematic evaluation of the internal consistency of the strategic postures and strategies being used or contemplated in the various areas should be performed.

A method for testing the internal consistency of an integrated strategic position is shown in Exhibit 8-3. By arraying the functional areas along both axes of a matrix, one can begin to identify the complementing and distracting relationships among the functions on either side of the diagonal. In an ideal situation, there would be no significant entries below the diagonal exhibiting weaknesses or redundancies, and all important relationships above the diagonal would be mutually reinforcing. By examining the various specific intersections, the strategist can greatly reduce the hazard of major oversights in scanning a complex network of interactions.

Summary

This brief chapter sums up the internal analyses of each business unit that should be performed as prescribed by the left side of the strategic planning system frameworks in Chapter 2. Having discussed the overall level of analysis in Chapter 3, we return to it in this chapter to reinforce the need for integration and to discuss analyses that can be performed only after substantial data analysis in the functional areas.

For instance, PIMS, which provides potentially useful overall insights into the strategic position of a business unit, requires the gathering of extensive data about many aspects of the business's operations. If this is done at a superficial level, the resulting analysis is likely to reflect the GIGO (Garbage In–Garbage Out) phenomenon that has become associated with computer studies. On the other hand, if PIMS data collection is treated as an element of the internal analyses discussed in the preceding five chapters, it can be a valuable aid in understanding a business unit's position. Indeed, many firms have found that the primary value of PIMS lies in the process that must be undertaken rather than in the PIMS products.

The same is true for the other integrated analyses discussed here. Any such analysis presumes the existence of a sophisticated level of understanding concerning the functional areas and their interrelationships. Such understanding can be developed only through the sorts of analyses discussed in Chapters 3–8. If overall and integrated analyses of anything other than a preliminary nature (as discussed in Chapter 3) are based on less than a firm foundation, they are likely to be misleading.

Notes

1. R. D. Buzzell, B. T. Gale, and R. G. M. Sultan, "Market Share: A Key to Profitability," *Harvard Business Review*, January-February, 1975, pp. 97–106; and R. D. Buzzell and F. D. Wiersema, "Modeling Changes in Market Share: A Cross-Sectional Analysis," *Strategic Management Journal*, January-March, 1981, pp. 27–42.

2. For a thorough discussion of the pros and cons of using cross-sectional models such as PIMS in strategic planning, see the following articles in *Planning Review*: Bradley T. Gale, "Planning for Profit," January, 1978, pp. 4–7, 30–32; Thomas H. Naylor, "PIMS: Through a Different Looking Glass," March, 1978, pp. 15–16, 32; and Bradley T. Gale, "Cross-Sectional Analysis: The New Frontier in Planning," March, 1978, pp. 17–20. See also Richard P. Rumelt and Robin Wensley, "In Search of the Market Share Effect," Academy of Management, San Diego, August, 1981.

3. Ralph Biggadike, "The Risky Business of Diversification," *Harvard Business Review*, May-June, 1979, pp. 103–111; and *Corporate Diversification: Entry, Strategy, and Performance* (Boston: Harvard Business School, 1979).

4. Carolyn Y. Y. Woo and Arnold C. Cooper, "Strategies of Effective Low Share Businesses," *Strategic Management Journal*, July–September, 1981, pp. 301–318.

5. Robert H. Hayes and Steven C. Wheelwright, "The Dynamics of Process-Product Life Cycles," *Harvard Business Review*, March-April, 1979, pp. 127–136; and "Link Manufacturing Process and Product Life Cycles," *Harvard Business Review*, January-February, 1979, pp. 133–140.

PART III

STRATEGIC ENVIRONMENTAL ANALYSIS

CHAPTER 9

Environmental Analysis

THE SPS FRAMEWORK of Chapter 2 (Exhibits 2-3 and 2-5) prescribes assessments of the general, operating, and internal environments. The internal environment assessments were discussed in detail in Chapters 3–8. Here and in the following chapter we turn to the assessments of the external environment that are so critical to effective strategic management.

In this chapter, we focus attention both on the role of environmental analysis in planning at the business unit level and on a general approach to formulating and performing the environmental analyses that must be done. In Chapter 10, we discuss a number of specific tools and techniques that can be applied in the conduct of the analyses.

This chapter is divided into three major parts. First, the role of environmental analysis in planning is discussed in terms of how environmental analyses answer four basic issues of strategic management. Then, an operational framework for performing environmental analyses is presented. Finally, the concept of an environmental information system—to provide the basic information to support environmental analyses—is discussed.

The Role of Environmental Analysis in Planning

One of the most straightforward views of planning is that it is a four-step process that involves the generation of detailed and carefully considered answers to four basic questions:

1. Where are we now?
2. Where do we want to be in the future?
3. What might prevent us from getting there?
4. What should we do to get from where we are now to where we want to be?

111

The organization that takes this view of planning must perform environmental analyses to adequately answer each of the four planning questions. The analyses must reflect:

1. Assessments of the current state of the environment and the role of the organization in it.
2. Projections and assessments of future environments, the environmental opportunities to be presented, and desirable future roles to be played.
3. Forecasts of environmental constraints that will inhibit (or enhance) the achievement of goals.
4. Predictions of the environmental impacts and consequences of the strategies and actions being contemplated.

Environmental analysis therefore focuses on realistically and comprehensively describing the current environment, projecting future ones, foreseeing environmental changes so that unhappy surprises may be avoided, and preventing unanticipated consequences of strategies and actions.

Assessing the Current Environment

Many individuals and organizations operate with limited or unrealistic perceptions of their environment. This is particularly true of organizations' perceptions of their image as it exists in the minds of clientele.

Analyses of an organization's image as it is perceived in the internal environment and in the operating environment often show great dissonance. For instance, the firm whose managers perceive it as producing a "high-quality product that demands a premium price" may be perceived by its customers as merely selling overpriced products. The high-level executive who sees himself or herself as "involved with customers" may well be viewed as "hobnobbing only with the bigwigs" by persons in the customer's organization who are of crucial importance in purchase decision making. Such differences of opinion may reflect genuinely different standards of comparison or expectation, but, on the other hand, they may represent institutionalized biases that reflect the ways buyers and sellers are paid to think and act. For example, few salespeople are trained to think of their products as being overpriced, and few purchasing personnel are expected to think of paying "premium prices for premium goods." As Howard Stevenson[1] and others have emphasized, the objectivity of managers and analysts in assessing their organizations' competencies is influenced by functional position, hierarchical level, backgrounds, and other personal factors.

EXHIBIT 9-1
Industry Sector Analysis Framework
Partial Illustration: Metal Containers

Material suppliers	Container fabricators	Customers
Steel		Brewing°
U.S. Steel		Anheuser-Busch
Bethlehem		Olympia
Others		Others
Glass		Soft-drinks
PPG		Pepsi-Cola
Brockway		Coca-Cola
Others		Others
Plastic	American Can	Oil
DuPont	Continental Can	Exxon
Dow	National Can	Phillips
Others	Crown Cork & Seal	Others
Aluminum	Campbell Soup	Cosmetics°
Alcoa	Reynolds Aluminum	Max Factor
Kaiser	Aerosol Techniques	Helena Rubenstein
Reynolds	Others	Others
Others		Food
Fiber		H. J. Heinz
Weyerhauser		Campbell Soup
Georgia Pacific		Others
Others		Pharmaceuticals°
		Eli Lilly
		Merck
		Others

° In the case of certain "hard to hold" products, contract packagers or fillers combine the containers and contents. For a thorough discussion of this industry sector, see "Aerosol Techniques, Inc.," Intercollegiate Case Clearing House #6-313-155.

Economic factors within the industry sector or operating environment can often be deciphered in terms of a framework similar to that in Exhibit 9-1, which deals with metal containers from the perspective of Crown Cork & Seal's metal fabrication activity. In Exhibit 9-1, the strength potential competitors derive from forward or backward integration is shown horizontally.

In order to illustrate the potential use of this framework, let us take a moment to examine the motives that newcomers might have for entering the market.

Technological innovations and cost pressures are among the common factors attracting newcomers to an industry. If we review the sources of horizontal and vertical competition surrounding Crown Cork & Seal Company in Exhibit 9-1, we see strong competition among major raw material suppliers who are seeking shares of a multibillion-dollar market. While each of these firms is seeking to maximize its share of market for a given raw material, such as aluminum, it is also at least implicitly competing with a substitute product against steel, plastic, and other materials. In this particular illustration, a major aluminum producer chose to integrate forward into can manufacturing because the existing container fabricators were unwilling (or unable) to work with aluminum satisfactorily. On the other hand, Campbell Soup threatened to set an example for many major customers by integrating backward to ensure a stable supply of cheap, standardized soup cans. In short, failure to meet technical challenges from one direction and price requirements from another set the stage for increased competition within the ever-evolving packaging industry.[2]

Organizations may be unaware of other important elements of their environment as well. One study has shown that regulatory information is almost uniformly regarded to be of major importance by high-level corporate executives. Few companies, however, have developed organized systems for dealing with regulatory data, and few general managers believe themselves or their organizations to be on top of such information.[3]

Projecting and Assessing Future Environments

Most organizations recognize the need to make assessments of the future environments they may face. Indeed, there is probably a wider recognition of the need to formally forecast some aspects of the future than there is a recognition of the need to formally assess the current environment.

In organizational planning, the role played by assessments of future environments is complex; it involves the strategic choice of the relative desirability of various alternative futures, the determination of environmental opportunities that should be pursued, and a selection of the overall role to be played by the organization in the environments of the future.

In this sense, the assessment of future environments becomes proactive. It is not merely projecting what will inevitably occur, but rather involves the choice of alternative futures to be, in part, created by the organization. As well, it involves the choice of those opportunities to be pursued and assessments of alternative roles to be played. This view of assessing the future, rather than the simple forecasting-oriented one, probably needs to be further developed in most organizations.

114

A particularly important aspect of the future operating environment for most organizations is the projection of industry sector profitability. Here, many helpful concepts can be borrowed from the field of economics.[4] Perhaps the predominant and most general factor to be considered is the expected level of rivalry within the sector. Although the definition of a relevant competitive sector is often quite difficult, our interest is in groups of firms offering products and/or services that are recognizable substitutes for one another. Rivalry, or the aggressiveness of competitive behavior, is in part influenced by the possible rewards of preemptive action tempered by the probability of success. In capital intensive markets, for example, high operating leverage may promise high returns on small increases in volume. On the other hand, a market for products with high variable costs may not provide particularly strong incentives, because the marginal returns would be modest. The future rivalry in an industry will be further affected by the size mix of the competitors. If two or three major firms dominate many small ones, the competitive forces are apt to be less severe than if six or eight firms of roughly comparable size are competing in the market. A final major issue influencing rivalry has to do with the time required for participants to perceive and respond to changes in competitive behavior. If changes in strategy are quite transparent and resources are fairly flexible, the ability of competitors to respond effectively will be greatly enhanced.

Another set of economic factors that should be considered when attempting to assess future opportunities for market success involves the barriers to entry into and exit from an industry. Barriers may include financial investment, access to technology, tariff restrictions, or efficiency of distribution system deployment. If these factors deter entry and demand is expected to remain strong, then future profitability may reasonably be predicted to be strong. If, on the other hand, demand may stabilize or decline and exit barriers are high, then industry profits may deteriorate drastically as inefficient participants strive to retain some market position through marginal cost-based pricing. The cardboard box industry, for example, has seen periods when this form of behavior has undermined profits on an industry-wide basis.

When analysts foresee possible evidence of the simultaneous alteration in several barriers to entry and/or exit, the resulting volatility can provide opportunities for rapid growth or possible bankruptcy. Traditional examples can be found in industries as diverse as electronic components, watches, and alcoholic beverages. The dramatic shifts in the apparel industry[5] capture almost all the variables from fashion, to technology, to international trade, whereas the shake-out

115

among the brokerage houses has been influenced mostly by a single variable—deregulation in markets and prices.[6]

The process of assessing the future environment has been described here as a proactive, anticipatory one. Such a posture is particularly important as one studies differential effects of environmental trends that extend from demographics to government regulation.[7]

This aspect of environmental assessment may be thought of as equivalent to the establishment of objectives for the organization. However, when they are cast in this environmental context, the objectives are more comprehensive and sophisticated than those that normally evolve from planning exercises. Objectives are stated in terms of roles and scenarios rather than as simple numerical goals. Such objectives can provide a better basis for substantive organizational change. Simpler objectives usually lead to future postures that are merely extrapolations or perturbations of past ones.

Forecasting Environmental Constraints

The most important role of forecasting is not projecting the future that will occur, but rather projecting possible environmental phenomena that might significantly constrain the organization in attaining its objectives or that might prevent the objectives from being achieved.[8] Of course, forecasts may show future factors that will be favorable to the achievement of objectives. However, since such positive factors are normally incorporated into the determination of the objective, the third step in the planning process is most effective when it focuses on inhibitors. This logical framework serves to ensure that managers or planners are not so enthralled with an objective and its rationale that they omit consideration of potential negative influences on the achievement of the objective.

One means for visualizing the future importance of environmental factors on an industry segment is through the use of a framework similar to that in Exhibit 9-2. From this exhibit we can see that environmental forces constitute important constraints in free or purely competitive markets and a dominant influence in monopolistic or regulated markets. Segmented markets seem to offer strategists the greatest opportunity to exercise organizational discretion. Therefore, one important leading indicator of the influence of environmental forces on an organization may be an assessment of the direction and rate of movement along the horizontal or industry characteristics axis. This form of analysis may yield rather pessimistic conclusions regarding size of the sphere for strategy making in industries as diverse as electrical utilities, hospitals, and telecommunications; however, managers may increasingly become expected to take the

EXHIBIT 9-2

Industry Characteristics as
Influencers of Strategic Discretion

same aggressive, proactive steps to interact profitably with environmental forces, which have traditionally been viewed largely as constraints, as they have to interact with customers and competitors.

Forecasts such as these are commonly made for a variety of both strategic and operational purposes. The techniques for making them are diverse, ranging from simple numerical extrapolations to sophisticated Delphi processes for obtaining and aggregating expert judgment[9] and formalized environmental paradigms.[10]

Predicting the Consequences of Alternative Strategies

One of the most important, and least developed, aspects of environmental assessment is that of predicting the probable consequences or impact of strategies that are being considered. This sort of prediction is often referred to in terms of "What if?" questions. The planner wishes to know the most likely consequence of taking a particular contemplated action. Sophisticated prediction of such consequences must go beyond simplistic numerical assessments such as revenue and profit levels to incorporate market shares, competitive behavior, second-order impacts, and similar factors.

Within the operating environment, one may be able to execute a three-step analysis to test the consequences of alternative strategies. First, one can develop a structure for the relevant environment that includes both the direct commercial relationships (as in Exhibit 9-1) and the indirect environmental interest groups or claimants (as discussed in the next section). A second step would be to forecast the market share, cash flow, and ROI consequences with the help of an

117

industry forecasting model. The final step in the first iteration would then be to integrate the forecasted results into the corporate strategy of the firm to see if they were satisfactorily consistent with and supportive of overall objectives. The second-order effects would have to be derived in the next iteration from expectations regarding competitors' and claimants' responses to the firm's actions.

Analyzing secondary effects The analysis of secondary effects is becoming more important as organizations increase the sophistication and effectiveness of their strategic planning activities. Firms must begin to expect responses not only from direct competitors but from other outside influencers as well. For example, corporations that pursued aggressive international expansion in the post–World War II era witnessed the reactions of foreign governments to what they often described as "capitalistic imperialism." Later, those firms that devoted themselves to growth through acquisition were favored but then disdained by the investment community, and shortly thereafter by the Federal government. More recently, the macroeconomists who provide forecasts for planners have begun to revise their models to compensate for the strategic behavior of firms in key sectors of the economy.

The same economists who influence corporate planners also influence governmental policy, so the environmental changes extend from the operating to the general environment. In the same sphere, Federal judges have responded to the increasing economic and statistical complexity of more and more of their cases by attending special seminars in economic theory and social welfare. This complexity in turn has resulted in large part from acquisitions and international trade stimulated by strategic planning. The immediate relevance of judges' concerns for a firm's environmental analysis function can be seen in the following brief quotations:

> So Demsetz (an economics professor) urged the judges to broaden their minds, almost literally—to think not of a beer market or a soft-drink market but of a market for liquid refreshments; to think not of cane sugar or beet sugar but of a sweetener market.

> As one judge asked: "What are tough for us are just these kinds of cases where defining a market is so important—aluminum versus copper wire, for example. What's your wisdom on that?"[11]

The legal environment is but one aspect of the general environment that deserves attention. John Rosenblum has developed a framework for environmental analysis at the level of individual countries that divides variables among three categories: (1) socioeconomic context, (2) governmental development strategy, and (3) performance.[12] From this perspective, governmental agencies are viewed as active agents whose performance should be explicitly considered in the assessment of the general environment. Needless to say, regardless of how active a planner views other participants in the environment to be, that planner must be prepared to modify assumptions, analyses, or corporate directions in order to avoid negative consequences from other players in the environment.

Thus, except in the case of superficial predictions that are generally meant to be only first-pass attempts at culling out obviously bad strategies, planners will wish to have their strategic decisions supported by comprehensive answers to a set of "What if?" questions. By obtaining these answers they can ensure that they are making the best possible use of currently available environmental data in the support of their strategic decision making.

An Environmental Assessment Process

William King and David Cleland[13] have developed a process of *claimant analysis* that can be adapted to provide a basic framework for addressing the environmental issues in each of the four basic planning phases.[14] The framework involves a series of steps:

1. Identifying claimants and their claims.
2. Refining the basic claimant definitions.
3. Assessing claims.
4. Using the claimant analysis in establishing objectives.

Identification of Claimants and Their Claims

The first step in using a claimant approach to establishing organizational purposes and directions is identifying claimant groups. Claimants are individuals, groups, or institutions that have a demand for something due from the organization.

Ordinarily, only a few individuals at most need be considered explicitly. For instance, a primary stockholder or a retired chief executive may have such influence that it would be propitious to identify the individual and to explicitly consider his or her claim. Normally, claimant groups—groups of individuals who are relatively homogeneous with regard to the demands that they place on the organization—will be of prime concern.

119

Exhibit 9-3 shows one way of identifying claimant groups and the nature of their claims on the business firm. Such a claimant model may be of direct use in planning in that it can serve as a checklist for managers to use in testing and evaluating proposed objectives or actions. Although this may seem to be an innocuous use of such a formidable-sounding entity as a claimant model, often a firm's decisions do not consider the possible consequences of its actions on its diverse clientele, simply because of the diversity and people's notorious inability to think of everything.

Undoubtedly, one illustration of this was Bristol-Myers Company's 1975 strategy of introducing a nonaspirin pain remedy called Datril on the basis of the product being as effective as, but lower priced than, the established product, Tylenol. When Tylenol maker Johnson & Johnson reacted with price cutting, deals, and aggressive sales promotion, Datril's price and novelty-factor advantages were rapidly overcome. Failure on the part of Bristol-Myers to foresee these reactions of the competitive claimant led to an upsetting of the market and a lack of anticipated success for the new product.[15]

Refining the Basic Claimant Model

Once the basic claimant structure has been developed, it can be refined on the basis of the relative homogeneity of various groups incorporated into the model. The claimant groups should be identified in terms of the homogeneity of their outlook, claims, and perceptions, rather than on their common legal status. For instance, although all stockholders of a given class have the same legal claims, they do not behave homogeneously. Speculators have very different planning horizons from conservative investors such as the proverbial little old widow who holds her stock to pass it on to her children. With respect to their claims on the firm, one is looking at the short term and the other at the long term, and this leads them to desire very different actions of the corporation. A stark example of the adverse consequences of failing to "refine the claimant model" appeared in a minority shareholder's judgment against Canadian Pacific Ltd., a judgment that may eventually reach $1 billion. The judge concurred with a single shareholder's assertion that CP was misappropriating the assets of a firm in which it held controlling interest.[16]

Similarly, customers and potential customers do not behave uniformly; nor do they respond uniformly to corporate sales strategies. This has been recognized in the concept of a market segment, which is widely used as a basis for marketing strategy development. Each of the wide array of different autos designed in Detroit and other automotive capitals around the world is targeted toward a particular

EXHIBIT 9-3

Claimant Structure for a Business Corporation

Claimant	Nature of the Claim
Operating Environment	
Stockholders	Participation in distribution of profits, election of board of directors, etc.
Creditors	Participation in interest payments and return of principal. Participation in certain management and owner prerogatives if certain restrictive covenants are violated.
Employees	Economic, social, and psychological satisfaction in the place of employment. Freedom from arbitrary and capricious behavior on the part of company officials. Share in fringe benefits and freedom to participate in collective bargaining.
Union	Recognition as the negotiating agent for the employees. Opportunity to perpetuate the union as a participant in the business organization.
Customers	Service provided the product, technical data to use the product, suitable warranties, spare parts to support the product during customer use.
Supplier	Continuing source of business, timely consummation of trade credit obligations, professional relationship in contracting for purchasing and receiving goods and services.
Competitors	Norms established by society and the industry for competitive conduct. Business statesmanship on the part of contemporaries.
Local Communities	Place of productive and healthful employment in the local community. Participation of the company officials in community affairs, regular employment, fair play, purchase of a reasonable portion of products in the local community, interest in and support of local government, support of cultural and charity projects.
General Environment	
Governments	Taxes (income, property, etc.), fair competition, and adherence to the letter and intent of public policy dealing with the requirements of "fair and free" competition. Legal obligation of businesspeople (and business organizations) to obey antitrust laws.
Citizenry	Participation in and contribution to the governmental process of society as a whole, creative communications between governmental and business units designed for reciprocal understanding, acceptance of a fair proportion of the burden of government and society. Fair price for products and advancement of the state of the art in the technology that the product line offers.

Source: Adapted from *Management: A Systems Approach* by D. I. Cleland and W. R. King, Copyright © 1972 by McGraw-Hill Book Company. Used with the permission of McGraw-Hill Book Company.

121

market segment that is relatively homogeneous with regard to the needs fulfilled by a car. Of course, this targeting does not always work. For instance, American Motors's introduction of the Pacer in 1975 resulted in initial sales to a market segment that was significantly older, more affluent, and better educated, than that which had been targeted. In much the same way, an early IBM computer designed for a few large firms with complex computation tasks was instead widely adopted for use as a high-speed adding machine and bookkeeping device.

The basic claimant structure can be expanded, as in Exhibit 9-4, to show various classes of stockholders and creditors as well as different employee groups and customer segments. As the hypothetical relationships demonstrate, claimant subgroups may have conflicting attitudes toward a given dimension of a firm's activities, and their perspectives toward various dimensions may not be easily reconcilable. Nonetheless, such a structured approach to claimant analysis should serve to highlight those critical relationships across which tradeoffs must be made.

EXHIBIT 9-4

Claimant Analysis Framework
(with hypothetical relationships)

	Organizational dimension			
Claimant groups	Dividend payments	Working conditions	Financial stability	New product innovation
Stockholders				
Pension funds	Desire	Indifferent	Important	Indifferent
Speculators	Indifferent	Indifferent		Critical
Firm's executives	Oppose	Important	Important	
Other				
Employees				
Part-time	Oppose	Indifferent	Indifferent	Indifferent
Unionized		Important	Important	Opposed
Executive		Important	Critical	Important
Creditors				
Bondholders	Indifferent	Indifferent	Critical	Cautious
Trade creditors			Important	Indifferent
Employees				
Customers				
Capital equipment	Indifferent	Indifferent	Important	Opposed or important
Consumer goods			Indifferent	Indifferent
Others				

Assessing Claims

Of critical importance to the utilization of a claimant structure as anything more than a general guide or checklist is the definition of measures, direct or proxy, for the claims of claimant groups. Indeed, measurability is one of the keys to the development of useful objectives in any situation, since measures permit the assessment of progress toward the accomplishment of objectives.

Each of the claims specified in the refined claimant structure should be analyzed with a view to defining objective measures of that claim. Some of these measures are straightforward: the amount of dividends, the time pattern of dividends, and the proportional payout of earnings may measure the stockholders' claim of participating in the distribution of profits.

However, some measures are much less apparent. Many organizations state objectives in terms of the way in which they wish to be perceived. For instance, one of PPG Industries's objectives has been reported to be "to have the company accepted (by the general public) as a dynamic responsible professionally managed corporation . . . ." This suggests a claim of the general public, but how can it possibly be measured? The answer, of course, is that it cannot be measured in the same sense that earnings or dividends can be. However, the tremendous strides in attitude measurement[17] in recent years provide the basis for the objective assessment of attitudes on numerical scales that can be traced over time to indicate whether progress is being made in achieving desired public image objectives.

The same approaches can be used with the customer (for firms that do not sell to individual consumers) and other clientele groups. For instance, one firm conducted an image survey of its primary customers in terms of a variety of dimensions related to customer perceptions of the firm's product, prices, personnel, practices, and other factors. When it was discovered that customer perceptions differed greatly from what had been anticipated, this survey led to significant changes in the firm's organization, assignment of duties, and procedures for preparing proposals for customer review. The impact of these and other strategic changes was monitored over time with additional surveys to assess progress in changing customer perceptions. It should be recognized, of course, that similar measures are required in conjunction with the PIMS data base (Chapter 8) for attributes such as product quality.

Proxy measures will also be appropriate to measure progress toward some organizational objectives. For instance, R. L. Ackoff[18] suggests that an improved employee relations or morale objective should be assessed in terms of proxies such as attrition rate, absenteeism, and productivity. If such objective proxies are complemented with attitude measures, a complete picture of progress toward the achievement of a morale objective may be obtained. Fortunately, however, an increasing number of major corporations are strengthening their staffs of environmental analysts and providing such specialists with greater access to the strategic planning process.[19]

Using the Claimant Analysis in Establishing Objectives

It can reasonably be argued that every objective of an organization must necessarily be related to one or more of the objectives of the organization's clientele. If the clientele analysis is comprehensive, it encompasses all of those who have a claim on the organization, and it thereby reflects all that the organization is about and all that it should be seeking.

In effect, under this view, an organization's objectives are derived from the diverse objectives and claims of its clientele. Of course, since the objectives and claims of various clientele groups are in conflict, choices must be made, and priorities must be applied to the broad array of claims. Edwin Murray has conceptualized these relationships in terms of a *negotiation framework* that draws these external exchange relationships into the strategic planning choice processes of the firm.[20]

The clientele analysis provides the basic data required for any rational choice process concerning objectives. In the absence of such an analysis, important claimants are likely to be overlooked or misunderstood, and thus the organization may adopt objectives and strategies that may cause unforeseen difficulties.

Environmental Information Systems

Systems and Subsystems

William King and David Cleland,[21] as well as others,[22] have designed and developed environmental information systems that can complement the organization's more familiar internally oriented information systems. Such systems are important to the conduct of effective environmental analysis on a continuing basis in the firm, because the worth of such analysis depends so directly on the availability of relevant environmental information.

The environmental information systems framework is shown in Exhibit 9-5. It is directly based on the four key planning questions

124

EXHIBIT 9-5

Input-Output Subsystem Structure
of the Environmental Information System

Information Uses (Outputs)	Subsystems	Information Sources (Inputs)
1. Situation assessment (What is the current situation?)	Internal operations Customers Image	Internal sources Present customers Other external sources (economic, techno- logical, etc.)
2. Goal development (What do we want the future situation to be?)	Potential customers Goals and policies	Potential customers Internal sources
3. Constraint identifica- tion (What con- straints might inhibit us?)	Competition Regulatory	Competitors Government Other external sources
4. Choice or selection of strategies (What shall we do to achieve our goals?)	Forecasting Strategy evalua- tion Intelligence	Internal sources External sources

discussed earlier. Thus, it is a system framework that is in context with the planning process that is to be supported.

In the middle column of Exhibit 9-5 is a list of subsystems which serve to relate information sources to information uses. Thus, the exhibit describes an environmental information structure in terms of inputs, outputs, and the subsystems that transform information inputs into decision outputs.

The information sources in the right column of Exhibit 9-5 are not exhaustive, nor are they uniquely identified with the uses with which they are matched in the left column. However, there is a general tendency for them to be so related. For instance, most companies' assessments of the current situation will be focused on internal and customer sources of information. This is because the company and its customers are the prime determinants of the current situation. Sim- ilarly, competitors and government agencies provide the most sig- nificant constraints in such areas as pricing, new technology, and regulations within which business must be conducted. These infor- mation sources primarily provide constraint identification (Output 3). Recent research pertaining to the Freedom of Information Act (FOIA) and its use in strategic analysis has shown government rec-

125

ords to be an inexpensive data source that may yield valuable information regarding competitors' plans and regulators' decision processes.[23] It should be remembered, however, that regulations that appear as constraints to one set of firms may simultaneously create market opportunities for other firms, whether in mine safety, fire protection, or some other field.

The subsystem structure outlined in the middle column of Exhibit 9-5 suggests how an information system may be structured to collect and analyze the information inputs in ways that will usefully support the decision outputs. For instance, the internal information that is useful for assessing the existing situation is primarily provided by the internal operations (transaction processing) and management control subsystems. Other information, for example that concerning intangibles such as the image of the organization as perceived by its customers, may be provided by an image subsystem.

Exhibit 9-5 also shows that information on the goals to be sought comes from potential customers through a potential-customer subsystem and from internal sources through a goals and policies subsystem. The latter subsystem treats the goals of the organization—the subjective aspect inherent in all decision making—and the policies that serve to guide and constrain choice.

Constraint identification is similarly supported by subsystems dealing with the competitive and regulatory environments, which create the most significant limitations on action. The final choice of a strategy is supported by a forecasting subsystem and a strategy evaluation subsystem, which are supported by internal and external data sources. These subsystems aid in the overall assessment of the worth of proposed strategies and in the assessment of the risks that are inherent in each.

Finally, in the choice of a strategy, management must be aware of specific occurrences in the competitive marketplace. Have competitors just raised their prices? Are they likely to be introducing a new product in our product line next month? The answers to these specific questions can be obtained and processed through an intelligence subsystem.

The framework of Exhibit 9-5 is meant to be illustrative rather than exhaustive. It shows how a set of environmental information subsystems may be developed to support the environmental analysis phase of planning. Such a framework ensures that the informational support will be consistent with the planning process and its objectives. Without it, environmentally focused information systems are sometimes developed in a fashion that provides neither integration of information nor effective planning support.

126

To illustrate how this can occur, consider the case of a firm that developed a competitive data system that compiled and disseminated one-paragraph intelligence statements written by sales and technical personnel and stored in a computerized memory. These intelligence assessments were prepared after visits to client firms and contacts with competitors' personnel. The items in the data system were retrievable only through a "dump" of all items related to a particular competitor or a specific time period, or both. A systems audit showed that the system was not utilized to the degree that had been anticipated in the system proposal, that it was not integrated into any decision-making process, and that the lack of evaluation and assessment of items that were put into the system led to a great likelihood of managers drawing erroneous conclusions on the basis of the information supplied by the system. As a result of the audit, the system was promptly deactivated.

Recently published research has shown another example of the somewhat unexpected behavioral consequences of the receipt of important strategic data which could be incorporated into the environmental information subsystem. Managers who were provided with specific data in addition to that generally available regarding the economic and political environment for investment opportunities in Eastern European countries revised their "estimates of inconvenience" upward rather than downward, as solicitors of investment dollars had hoped.[24]

The system-subsystem structure of Exhibit 9-5 may imply use of sophisticated computerized information systems, but this need not be the case. Certainly, in the case of the image subsystem, the image data acquisition process is the most crucial element, and the required data analyses may be a relatively incidental part of the total process.

William King[25] provides detailed descriptions of actual systems corresponding to most of the subsystems in Exhibit 9-5. Not all such systems require computerization. Each, however, is a systematic set of procedures for acquiring, processing, and disseminating environmental information in a fashion that is relevant to, and an integral part of, the environmental analysis process.

Taxonomy of Environmental Information Systems

Liam Fahey and William King[26] have described three levels of environmental scanning systems that they found to exist in various organizations: irregular, regular, and continuous. Exhibit 9-6 shows the basis for distinguishing among these three environmental scanning system models.

The irregular model described in the first column of Exhibit 9-6 represents a process of ad hoc environmental study, which is likely stimulated by some unanticipated occurrence in the environment such as energy shortages or a competitor's introduction of a new product. It is largely a reaction to a crisis. The scanning focus is toward the past, and its intent is to identify the implications of an event that has already taken place. The emphasis is on immediate or short-term reactions to the crisis, and little attention is paid to identifying and evaluating future environmental trends and events.

The second model is more comprehensive and systematic. It entails a regular (usually annual) review of the environment, or at least those components of it that are deemed important. This system is typically decision- or issue-oriented. For example, what environmental changes would be likely to have an impact on a contemplated investment decision? It is also more future-oriented than the first

EXHIBIT 9-6

Taxonomy of Environmental Scanning
Systems

System characteristic	Irregular	Regular	Continuous
Media scanning activity	Ad hoc studies	Periodically updated studies	Structured data collection and processing systems
Scope of scanning	Specific events	Selected events	Broad range of environmental systems
Motivation for activity	Crisis-initiated	Decision- and issue-oriented	Planning process–oriented
Temporal nature of activity	Reactive	Proactive	Proactive
Time frame for data	Retrospective	Primarily current and retrospective	Prospective
Time frame for decision impact	Current and near-term future	Near-term future	Long-term future
Organizational makeup	Various staff agencies	Various staff agencies	Environmental scanning unit

Source: Adapted with permission from Liam Fahey and William R. King, "Environmental Scanning for Corporate Planning," *Business Horizons*, August, 1977, pp. 61–71.

approach, and it is proactive in the sense that relevant and current issues or decisions are identified and then the environment is analyzed to determine its future impact on them. Still, the focus is primarily retrospective in that attention is paid first to the current situation and then to simple extrapolations of the recent past into the near future. For instance, when an auto firm conducts annual studies of consumer preferences in auto safety and fuel economy for the purpose of determining appropriate advertising appeals for the already-developed cars of the next model year, the regular scanning model is being applied. Hence, the irregular and regular scanning models reflect differences in degree.

The third model manifests a clear distinction in kind. It emphasizes the continuous monitoring of various environmental systems—political, regulatory, competitive, and so on—rather than specific events. Its motivation and methods are systems-oriented in that regular organizational systems are used for both data processing and information utilization. For example, consumer studies conducted by an auto company analyzing preference trends among various market segments are used as direct input for design decisions on future models. Another firm monitors government regulatory activity—an environmental subsystem that has not proved to be crucial in the past—in order to influence the firm's future by lobbying against increased government regulation. In both examples, the firm's systems are performing in the continuous mode.

Perhaps most important from an operational point of view is the fact that continuous scanning must be organizationally structured. Unlike the irregular and regular models, in which studies may be left to the appropriate staff departments, the continuous systems approach requires, at a minimum, a scanning agency that functions as a central clearing house for environmental information. Computerized information systems dedicated to scanning activities may also be required.

Moreover, the continuous model necessitates a planning process viewpoint that integrates the information processing and information utilization functions for strategic analysis. While the other models provide environmental information to support specific choices, the continuous model supports the variety of choices inherent in strategic planning—from the selection of organizational missions and objectives to the choice of specific programs and funding commitments. Fahey and King found each of the three system models in existence in some firms that they studied. However, the continuous variety was clearly not well developed in many of the firms, despite the concern that most expressed that they were not adequately dealing with some

129

aspects of their environment due to poor or inadequate environmental information.

Summary

To complement the internal analyses of the firm and its potential comparative advantages, assessments of the external environment must also be made. This chapter deals with the general nature of these assessments in terms of four varieties of analysis, each having a specific role and purpose—assessments of the current state of the environment, projections of future environments, forecasts of constraints, and predictions of impacts and consequences.

The chapter also presents an environmental assessment process that may serve as the operational basis for performing these assessments. The approach is oriented toward assessing the claims that various "stakeholder" groups have on the firm as a basis for understanding, predicting, and influencing environmental relationships.

Since all environmental assessment requires that information be collected and analyzed, the idea of an environmental information system is introduced. Distinctions are made among various kinds of such systems to serve as a guide for their development.

Chapter 10 introduces a variety of specific techniques that may be used to implement the analyses discussed in this chapter.

Notes

1. Howard H. Stevenson, "Defining Corporate Strengths & Weaknesses," *Sloan Management Review*, Spring, 1976, pp. 51–68; and earlier in "Defining Corporate Strengths & Weaknesses: An Exploratory Study," unpublished doctoral dissertation, Harvard Business School, 1969.

2. More detailed descriptions may be found in "Crown Cork & Seal and the Metal Container Industry," Intercollegiate Case Clearing House #6-373-077.

3. Liam Fahey and William R. King, "Environmental Scanning for Corporate Planning," *Business Horizons*, August, 1977, pp. 61–71.

4. We are indebted to Michael E. Porter's analyses for some of the following concepts as found in "Note on the Structural Analysis of Industries," ICCH #9-376-054, and "How Competitive Forces Shape Strategy," *Harvard Business Review*, March-April, 1979, pp. 137–145.

5. "Apparel's Last Stand," *Business Week*, May 14, 1979, pp. 60–63, 66, 70.

6. Carol J. Loomis, "The Shake-Out on Wall Street Isn't Over Yet," *Fortune*, May 22, 1978, pp. 58–64, 66. Further insights into strategists' uses of entry barriers can be found in George S. Yip, "Barriers to Entry: A Corporate Strategy Perspective," unpublished dissertation, Harvard Business School, 1980.

7. For further details, see Robert A. Leone, *Environmental Controls: The Impact on Industry* (Lexington, Massachusetts: D. C. Heath and Company, 1976); or "The Real Costs of Regulation," *Harvard Business Review*, November-December, 1977, pp. 57–66.

8. For a formal explanation of the role of constraints in forming organizational objectives, see Herbert A. Simon, "On the Concept of Organizational Goal," *Administrative Science Quarterly*, vol. 9, 1964, pp. 1–22.

9. See, for example, Ronald D. Kennedy, "Usefulness of Futuristic Forecasts as a Planning Tool in Industry," unpublished doctoral dissertation, University of Pittsburgh, 1979.

10. Harold Klein, "Commentary," in *Strategic Management* (Boston: Little, Brown, 1979), pp. 144–151.

11. Walter Guzzardi, Jr., "Judges Discover the World of Economics," *Fortune*, May 21, 1979, p. 61. See further discussion in Walter Guzzardi, Jr., "A Search for Sanity in Antitrust," *Fortune*, January 30, 1978, p. 72.

12. John W. Rosenblum, "An Introduction to Environmental Analysis for Management," Intercollegiate Case Clearing House #1-378-101. An extended application of this analytical framework can be found in Bruce R. Scott, John W. Rosenblum, and Audrey T. Sproat, *Case Studies in Political Economy: Japan 1854–1977* (Boston: Harvard Business School, 1980).

13. William R. King and David I. Cleland, *Strategic Planning and Policy* (New York: Van Nostrand Reinhold, 1978), Chapter 7.

14. William King has shown how the basic claimant analysis process can be extended to functional levels of the organization. He develops illustrations for the information processing function in William R. King, "Strategic Planning for MIS," *MIS Quarterly*, March, 1978, pp. 27–37.

15. See "A Painful Headache for Bristol-Myers," *Business Week*, October 6, 1975, pp. 78–80.

16. "How a Lone Investor Stunned Canadian Pacific," *Business Week*, March 19, 1979, p. 124.

17. See G. F. Summers, *Attitude Measurement* (New York: Rand McNally, 1970).

18. R. L. Ackoff, *A Concept of Corporate Planning* (New York: Wiley, 1970), p. 30.

19. "The New Corporate Environmentalists," *Business Week*, May 28, 1979, pp. 154, 162.

20. Edwin A. Murray, Jr., "Strategic Choice as a Negotiated Outcome," *Management Science*, May, 1978, pp. 960–971.

21. William R. King and David I. Cleland, "Environmental Information Systems for Strategic Marketing Planning," *Journal of Marketing*, October, 1974, pp. 35–40.

22. Francis J. Aguilar, *Scanning the Business Environment* (New York: Macmillan, 1965); Warren J. Keegan, "Multinational Scanning: A Study of Information Sources Utilized by Headquarters Executives in Multinational Companies," *Administrative Science Quarterly*, September, 1974, pp. 411–421; Asterios Kefalas and Peter P. Schoderbek, "Scanning the Business Environment: Some Empirical Results," *Decision Sciences*, January, 1973, pp. 63–74; and Philip S. Thomas, "Environmental Scanning: The State of the Art," *Long Range Planning*, February, 1980, pp. 20–28.

23. David B. Montgomery, Anne H. Peters, and Charles B. Weinberg, "The Freedom of Information Act: Strategic Opportunities and Threats," *Sloan Management Review*, Winter, 1978, pp. 1–14.

24. Ion Amariuta, David P. Rutenberg, and Richard Staelin, "How American Executives Disagree about the Risks of Investing in Eastern Europe," *Academy of Management Journal*, March, 1979, pp. 138–151.

25. William R. King, *Marketing Management Information Systems* (New York: Van Nostrand Reinhold, 1977), Chapter 5.

26. Liam Fahey and William R. King, "Environmental Scanning for Corporate Planning," *Business Horizons*, August, 1977, pp. 61–71.

131

CHAPTER 10

Techniques for Environmental Assessment

THE OVERALL APPROACH to environmental assessment developed in Chapter 9 can be implemented using a wide variety of techniques. The purpose of this chapter is to review some of those that have proved most useful.

Unfortunately, no single technique has proved useful in addressing all of the phases of the environmental assessment process. Most are limited to, or primarily focused toward, one of the phases—the assessment of the current environment, the projection of desirable future environments, the forecasting of environmental constraints, or the prediction of the impacts of strategies.

In a single chapter one cannot deal with a wide variety of techniques in sufficient detail to give them meaning to the reader. Therefore, we have chosen to deal with some of the more basic, generic, and useful techniques for these four areas in detail and to relegate others to more limited coverage. Sufficient references are provided to make accessible those that are treated in less detail.

Techniques for Assessing the Current Environment

Environmental data that reflect the current environment are collected in some form by nearly every business firm. Unless such data are evaluated for relevance and significance, they may be a detriment, rather than an aid, to planning. This suggests the all-too-real caricature of the harried manager, surrounded by computer printouts, who has neither the time, energy, nor ability to read and digest this material, which in any case lacks the most important information. An excess of information is a particular problem in the environmental assessment area, where new information often turns out to be voluminous and it is often difficult to separate the relevant from the irrelevant, because all the information is unfamiliar.

Strategic Data Bases

William King and David Cleland have suggested the concept of a strategic data base (SDB) to overcome some of the difficulties in environmental assessment.[1] An SDB is developed as a part of the planning process. Strategic data bases are concise statements of the most significant items related to clientele or environments—those that affect the organization's strategic choices.

The evaluations of the vast quantities of data forming the raw input for the development of strategic data bases should be performed by task forces—teams of managers representing diverse interests within the organization. In this way, the organization can be assured that the evaluation does not represent one narrow point of view or only the parochial viewpoint of analysts.

These teams of *managers*, supported by staff, may be charged with arriving at conclusions concerning an *approximate specified number* (usually from ten to fifteen) of the *most important* factors affecting the future of the organization in a specified area.

Competition is one such area. Competitors who are identified to be outperforming the firm can be identified, and their significant actions and strategies can be cataloged and analyzed. Several major issues must be addressed with regard to competition:

1. Who are the several most threatening competitors?
2. What are the strengths and weaknesses of the competition?
3. What is believed to be the strategy (and associated risks) of the competition?
4. What resources (financial, plant and equipment, managerial know-how, marketing, and technical abilities) are at the competition's disposal to implement planned strategies?
5. Do any of these factors give the competition a distinctly favorable position?

Similar analyses may be developed for the key technologies with which the firm deals in its major markets, the firm's own strengths and weaknesses, key environmental issues, and other factors.

The importance of this simple SDB concept can be clarified by contrasting this participative process with the one more commonly used to prepare the information inputs to planning. The latter approach relies on staff analysts who gather data and prepare documents to serve as background information to support planning activi-

133

ties and choices. Because the planners and analysts who perform these tasks often have neither the managerial expertise nor the authority to make the significant choices involved in any information evaluation process, the typical output of such an exercise is a document that seems to have been prepared on the basis of "not leaving anything out."

This technique emphasizes ensuring that nothing relevant is omitted rather than distinguishing the most relevant information from the mass of the less relevant and the irrelevant. Thus, it only perpetuates the existing state of affairs regarding the informational support provided to managers at all levels: the manager is deluged with irrelevant information and at the same time is unable to find the most crucial elements of information.[2]

Conversely, the SDB process focuses on charging task forces, which are made up of managers representing various of the parochial interests within the organization, with gathering and evaluating the data in each of a number of areas and *choosing*—through the consensual process that guides most task force decision making—those that are the most important to the development of the organization's strategy.

Techniques for Assessing the Future Environment

The future environment may be assessed either as a given or as a dynamic entity to be influenced by the firm. The most common practice among business firms has been to treat the future environment as a fixed element that must be accommodated. The more proactive viewpoint—seeing the future as an entity that is, to some extent, under the firm's influence—is the focus of modern strategic planning.

When the uncontrollable view of the future is adopted, the environment is viewed as a constraint on the firm's actions; when the more proactive approach is taken, the environment is seen as something to be, in part, created. It is in this sense that the concept of alternative futures—among which choices are to be made—has come into prominence.

Alternative Futures

The constraint view of the future environment is often associated with descriptions of the future that are expressed in terms of a single variable, such as GNP, while the alternative futures approach discusses a number of variables and is more meaningful even in the case of a single variable. One may project a "most likely," pessimistic, and optimistic situation for future GNP and analyze strategies in terms of each. While the degree of control implicit in such a single aggregate description of the future is not as great as it might be in a more complex and less aggregated description, these alternative projections provide the basis for:

1. Analyzing the sensitivity of proposed strategies to the alternative futures.
2. Developing contingency plans to fit the alternative projections.
3. Developing trigger points that definitively specify when various contingencies have, in fact, occurred.

Sensitivity analysis The possibility of analyzing the sensitivity of various proposed strategies is one of the most important reasons to think of future projections in terms of a set of alternatives rather than a single fixed projection. It may be possible to find a robust strategy— one that produces good results under a variety of future environmental conditions. When the analysis of alternative projections shows that a particular strategy performs well under a wide range of possible futures, one can be relatively comfortable with it.

Contingency plans If no such strategy can be found, the notion of contingency plans comes into prominence. A contingency plan is simply an alternative to the basic plan, to be implemented if the anticipated future environment is not being realized. Thus, one might decide to adopt a "skim the cream" pricing strategy under the assumption that the future holds no significant new competitors for at least a year. A contingency plan, based on an alternative pessimistic future projection, might be to reduce price if another firm begins test marketing a competitive product within the year. Thus, with such a contingency plan, one is able to implement the chosen strategy (skim the cream) based on the likely future, while still retaining the ability to shift to a contingent strategy should the anticipated contingency occur.

Trigger points The trigger point is the clear and unequivocal environmental information that gives the signal to implement the contingency plan. Without one, it is easy to be lulled into complacency by a series of incremental changes from the anticipated chain of events. Thus, one might convince oneself that the competitor's actions taken today are not significant enough to warrant a change in the previously chosen plan. This may happen time after time. Without

135

the perspective of a previously selected trigger point clearly indicating that a cumulative set of environmental happenings is sufficiently significant to warrant a change, there is the danger that the manager, who is immersed in fighting day-to-day fires, will not recognize a contingency when it occurs. With a trigger point, the "red flag" is raised.

All of these actions may be taken within the framework of a fixed view of the future environment—a view of the future environment as a constraint with which the firm must cope. The more proactive view of the future environment provides an even richer opportunity for the specification of alternative futures.

Scenarios

A formulated sequence of future events, some controllable and some uncontrollable, represents a future scenario. Such scenarios permit one to analyze the possible consequences of a series of complex phenomena.

Although scenarios are often rather qualitative, they nonetheless can be detailed. They permit the integrated consideration of many diverse factors. A specific corporate mission and its associated strategy and programs may be explored in terms of a scenario involving societal change, competitive reactions, and regulatory change. The scenario thus provides a structure for considering the overall system in a way that few abstract techniques can hope to do.

The best known applications of scenarios are undoubtedly the work of Herman Kahn and D. Weiner, who applied them on a worldwide scope.[3] Scenarios have been used in organizational planning to explore the consequences of current choices of missions, objectives, strategies, and programs as they will affect and be affected by a complex environment. R. D. Zentner[4] summarized more than thirty articles on the subject, which discussed the use of scenarios in a variety of applications covering the role of management in dealing with governmental intervention, the seizure of Arab oil, bank assets and liabilities, the pulp and paper industry, world energy systems, and other topics. Since most uses of scenarios by business firms are proprietary, they appear infrequently in public literature, but firms such as General Electric, Monsanto, Shell Oil,[5] and Atlantic Richfield[6] are known to use them extensively. One of the most comprehensive sets of scenarios available for public scrutiny was prepared by the Stanford Research Institute (SRI) for the Environmental Protection Agency (EPA) in the early 1970s.

The alternative futures concept is implemented in its richest form when several distinct scenarios are developed. Through a process of positing significantly different alternative-future operating environments, managers are stimulated to think more openly and creatively about possible strategic roles for a corporation.[7]

Trend Extrapolation

One of the best known methods for forecasting the future is trend extrapolation. While the technique is most naïvely applied to a quantitative time series (for example, a past sales trend may be used to project future sales), other more sophisticated approaches are used in planning. For instance, in the area of technological forecasting, trends in productivity may be extrapolated into the future without regard to precisely how they may occur. This has been done with aircraft using time series of productivity measures such as ton-miles per hour and passenger-miles per hour and with illumination using a productivity measure of lumens per watt. The speed, weight, thrust, and other characteristics of aircraft have similarly been extrapolated from historical data for planning purposes.[8]

Trend extrapolation is equally feasible in other less quantitative areas. For instance, the social and political turbulences of the late 1960s and early 1970s demonstrated conclusively to public agencies and business firms that they needed improved capabilities for developing proactive strategies based on forecasts of social and political phenomena. In 1967, General Electric established sociopolitical forecasting as a separate organizational entity to meet this challenge.

One of the outputs of sociopolitical forecasting at General Electric is given by Ian H. Wilson in the form of a profile of significant value changes between 1969 and 1980. A version of his values profile is shown in Exhibit 10-1, which describes contrasting values (war versus peace or work versus leisure) that are held by trend setters in the general population.

Though now somewhat outdated, this profile was used by GE during the early 1970s to assess what the 1980s might hold in terms of the changing values of consumers. A similar analysis for the next decade would reveal obvious shifts in values among certain constituent or claimant groups, and it would thus provide important inputs to the claimant structures described in Exhibits 9-3 and 9-4.

Econometric Forecasting Models

Another type of large-scale model used by corporate strategic planners is the large-scale econometric model. Several firms, such as Data Resources, Inc., Chase Econometric Associates, Inc., and Wharton Econometric Forecasting Associates, Inc., operate such models

137

EXHIBIT 10-1

Values Profile

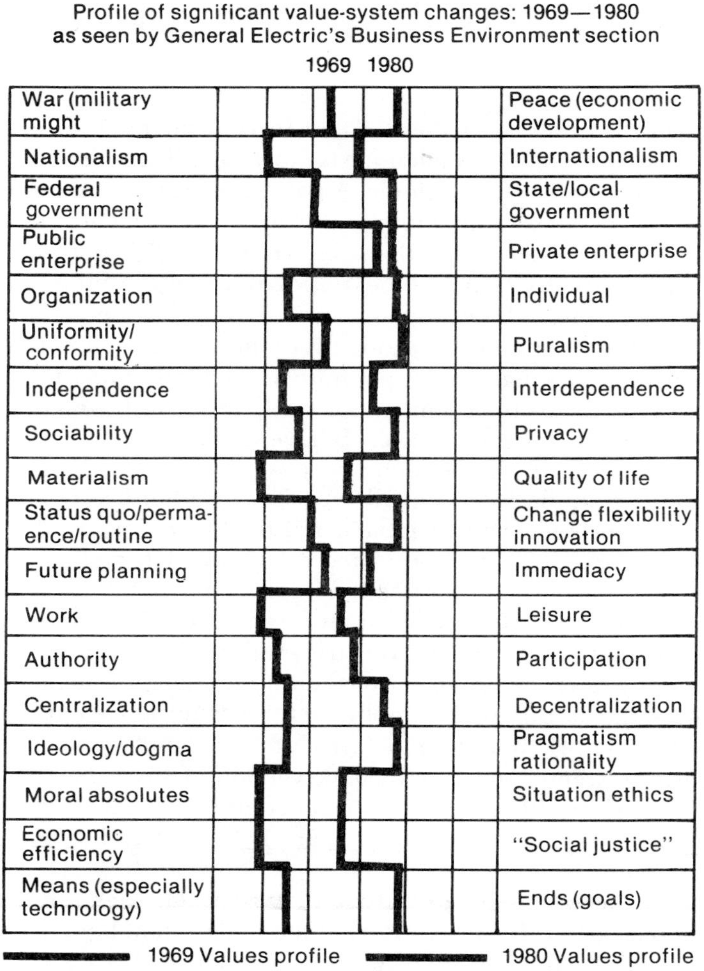

Profile of significant value-system changes: 1969—1980
as seen by General Electric's Business Environment section

1969 1980

War (military might		Peace (economic development)
Nationalism		Internationalism
Federal government		State/local government
Public enterprise		Private enterprise
Organization		Individual
Uniformity/conformity		Pluralism
Independence		Interdependence
Sociability		Privacy
Materialism		Quality of life
Status quo/permanence/routine		Change flexibility innovation
Future planning		Immediacy
Work		Leisure
Authority		Participation
Centralization		Decentralization
Ideology/dogma		Pragmatism rationality
Moral absolutes		Situation ethics
Economic efficiency		"Social justice"
Means (especially technology)		Ends (goals)

━━━━ 1969 Values profile   ━━━━ 1980 Values profile

Source: Ian H. Wilson, used with permission.

and provide forecasts and related services to businesses and other organizations on a fee basis. These econometric models depict the national economy in terms of hundreds of statistically estimated equations. The equations are based on economic theory as well as empirical evidence, and they are used to test the economy's likely response to national policy changes in such areas as tax rates, money supplies, and energy prices. In addition to econometric models, var-

138

ious firms operate industry input-output models that forecast special production indices or developments in specific segments of the economy.[9]

These forecasts can be used in organizational strategic planning activity in a variety of ways:

1. To develop a set of consistent forecasts for a variety of different products or markets.
2. To evaluate the impact of different national policy scenarios on the economic performance of various markets.
3. To evaluate the market segments that will significantly contribute to future growth.

Although such models are often spoken of in the terminology of "What if?" questions, the focus of the questions is different from the use of the term in this book. Aggregate econometric models have no direct capability for assessing the future impact of actions taken by a single organization, and this is the sense in which "What if?" questions are usually used. For example, "What would happen if we changed our prices?" The "What if?" question capability of econometric models operates at the aggregate level of national policy scenarios. For example, "What would happen if taxes were cut by 10 percent?" Although the latter sort of scenario can be a useful guide to corporate planners, these models will not provide "What if?" answers to corporate strategy issues.

Cross-Impact Matrices

The cross-impact matrix is another device for assessing future environments in a more complex fashion than is permitted by trend extrapolation. Cross-impact matrices may be used when several forecasts are believed to interact with one another. The matrix simply provides a systematic approach to tracing through chains of effects so that forecasts are not overly simplistic.

One environmental phenomenon that is being forecast may increase or decrease the likelihood of another occurring, may affect the timing of another, or may be causally related to another, thus ensuring that the second occurs or preventing it from occurring. These influences may also vary in both strength and timing.

The cross-impact matrix merely summarizes all of these relationships in a fashion such as that shown in Exhibit 10-2. The rows are labeled with three innovative technologies, T_1, T_2, and T_3, and the given probabilities of their being developed by the years indicated. The same three technologies are listed in the columns of the matrix. The body of the matrix shows the interactions.

EXHIBIT 10-2

Cross-Impact Matrix

Technologies (Probability, Year)	T_1	T_2	T_3
T_1 (0.9, 1989)		110% impact no time lag	must occur in 5 years
T_2 (0.8, 1995)	Precluded		must occur sometime
T_3 (0.6, 2000)	Precluded	-20% impact in 3 years	

Note: Entries above diagonal indicate effect if the earlier row event occurs; entries below diagonal indicate effect if the earlier column event does not occur.

For instance, consider the three entries at the top right. The effect of T_1 on T_2 is to enhance its occurrence by 110 percent with no time lag. If T_1 occurs, T_3 must occur in five years. Similarly, if T_2 occurs, T_3 must occur sometime.

The three entries at the lower left show the effect if the earlier column event *does not* occur. If T_1 does not occur, both T_2 and T_3 are precluded from happening. Nonoccurrence of T_2 will have a negative 20 percent impact on T_3 in three years.

This simple cross-impact illustration shows that the matrix is merely a way of keeping track of complex interactions. Other calculations may also be performed to enhance the technique's value, but even the basic application provides a good method of dealing with interacting environmental phenomena.

Delphi Forecasting

The basic forecasts that are an essential ingredient for cross-impact analysis may be obtained through the use of Delphi or other means. Delphi—the most widely used judgmental forecasting approach—is certainly not limited to being an aid in cross-impact analysis. Indeed this is a minor role for Delphi. However, the need to have basic forecasts of the future under specified conditions, as is the case in cross-impact analysis, illustrates the role that can be played by Delphi judgmental forecasting.

The Delphi forecasting approach was developed as a method of eliciting expert opinion about the future in a systematic fashion. Such opinion forecasts are familiar and valuable inputs to strategic planning. For instance, McGraw-Hill's surveys of businesses' plans for making expenditures on plant and equipment are published regularly in *Business Week* and are widely used as forecasting bases.

Other forecasts are made by obtaining the collective judgments of groups. However, forecasts based on composites of group opinions have often been found to represent compromises rather than consensuses, since the prestige or personality of certain individuals can inordinately influence the judgment of a group.

The Delphi technique enables a group of experts to contribute to one another's understanding and to refine their opinions as a result of interaction with other experts within the group. Delphi physically separates the experts, however, so that individuals and their rationales do not become submerged in the overt activities of a group.[10]

Delphi involves a series of steps:

1. Predictions by each expert.
2. Clarification by a neutral investigator.
3. Requestioning of experts combined with feedback from other experts.

The process of requestioning is designed to eliminate misinterpretation and to bring to the attention of each expert elements not known to all.

A typical Delphi session might involve an initial round in which each participant is asked to predict when a technological development is likely to occur. The predictions from the various participants are tabulated and clarified and then fed back to the participants in a second round. The experts are then asked to review their first predictions in the light of those of the other participants. Those who made extreme assessments (the upper and lower 25 percent of responses in the first round) are also asked to explain these extreme positions. The process may go on through a number of rounds in which each participant is given the opportunity to reassess his or her forecast in the light of those made by others and their rationales. Sometimes this results in a consensus developing around a well-rationalized but initially extreme position. At other times, the extremists moderate their forecasts. In any case, the difficulties of face-to-face forecasting are avoided, while the benefits of expert judgment are realized.

Brainstorming

Standing in marked contrast to the structured process of the Delphi technique is the free-form communications procedure known as brainstorming. (This face-to-face, interactive technique is intended to stimulate creative proposals.) Despite the absence of research supporting the validity (or even utility) of this methodology, it is a recognized approach to future assessment. Some firms have been using it for over a decade, and William Hall's research[11] regarding new venture initiation showed that most large corporations use some form of brainstorming as a means of stimulating ideas.

Brainstorming is one technique that may be used for group invention of alternative futures. If the approach is complemented with subsequent evaluation sessions, it can serve as a vehicle for introducing strategy-oriented debate into the organization.[12]

System Simulation

The best-known varieties of futuristic forecasting are the large-scale simulation models such as those reported on by Dennis Meadows et al. in *The Limits to Growth*.[13] These models depict the world as a system, incorporating consideration of population; technological, industrial, and natural resources; and other interacting subsystems. The models project the consequences of current interacting subsystems and growth rates into the future. Thus, they permit the analysis of the impact of global growth policies. The initial and widely publicized study reported on in *The Limits to Growth* indicated that if the world did not moderate industrial and population growth, the world system might well collapse within fifty years.

Subsequent studies[14] have altered this bleak outlook to some degree. However, the various forecasts have had great impact, if only in a psychological sense, on the general populace and on organizational strategic planning. In general, large-scale simulation models of the world economy have great potential for providing important informational inputs to the strategic planning of business firms and government agencies.

Techniques for Evaluating Alternative Futures

The most important phase of environmental assessment is that which focuses on the evaluation of alternative futures and of the strategies that are implicit in each alternative future.

Policy Delphi

One means of refining analyses that develop from the comparison of alternative scenarios is the Policy Delphi.[15] In situations where no single optimal solution can be found, this version of the Delphi technique seeks to explore opposing personal interpretations of data by developing the strongest possible opposite points of view on policy issues. Policy Delphis have been reported in conjunction with analyses of several public sector issues, but they have received very little published attention in the business context.

Dialectic Policy Analysis

Another potentially valuable approach to strategy formulation that makes use of opposing viewpoints was developed by Richard Mason.[16] Unlike the Policy Delphi, which, like all Delphis, relies on non-face-to-face communication, Mason's system uses a face-to-face communication technique to analyze the different assumptions that must prove to be valid if each of two opposing strategies is to be effective. Acting as a consultant to the RMK Abrasives Company, he took opposing strategies and analyzed them with respect to their underlying assumptions. In doing so, he reportedly produced a level of understanding that would have been difficult to achieve otherwise.

Vulnerability Analysis

A framework for assessing the impacts of various environmental factors on the viability of the enterprise has been developed by Douglas Hurd and Riggs Monfort.[17] Their vulnerability assessment diagram, as depicted in Exhibit 10-3, forces the analyst to specify both the magnitude of impact and the probability of occurrence. By placing events that are important to the future of the firm at the appropriate locations on the matrix, analysts and executives can separate them into classes (labeled here A, B, and C) depending on their criticality to the organization. The firm is then in a position to expend time and resources in proportion to the severity of the perceived threat. If a particular problem cannot be eliminated, action can often be taken to reduce either the magnitude of effects or the probability of occurrence, in order to lessen the overall corporate vulnerability.

Corporate Simulation Models

Another simulation model, distinct from those that have been developed largely as forecasting devices, is the corporate model. Corporate models attempt to portray a complex organization and its environmental interactions. In a survey, G. W. Gershefski[18] reported the various uses to which corporate models were being put:

1. Evaluating alternative operating or investment strategies.
2. Providing revised financial projections rapidly.
3. Assisting in determination of feasible corporate goals.

EXHIBIT 10-3

Vulnerability Assessment Diagram

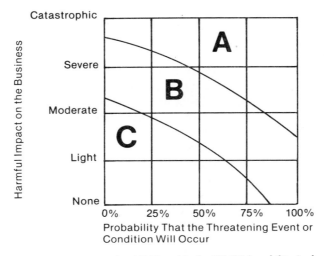

Source: Douglas A. Hurd and E. Riggs Monfort III, "Vulnerability Analysis: A New Way to Assess Future Trends," *Planning Review*, November, 1979, p. 33. Reprinted with permission from *Planning Review*, a bi-monthly journal of the North American Society for Corporate Planning, 1406 Third National Building, Dayton, Ohio 45402.

4. Analyzing the effect of interacting items.
5. Determining the sensitivity of earnings to external factors.
6. Developing a documented projection of financial position.
7. Allowing management to consider more variables when planning.
8. Determining the need for long-term debt.
9. Validating manually prepared projections and existing procedures.
10. Developing a corporate data base or information system.
11. Assisting in the evaluation of capital investment proposals.

   A more recent survey[19] identified only three total corporate simulation models that had been completely implemented. However, less-detailed model versions have been used to emphasize specific major aspects of the overall enterprise. For instance, P. Kotler describes an approach that emphasizes the marketing sector of the business, and J. B. Boulden and E. S. Buffa[20] describe a computerized approach that emphasizes production relationships in an overall corporate model. In each case, the segment of the business that is emphasized is treated in detail, whereas other segments are treated at a high level of aggregation and abstraction. A model such as Kotler's therefore permits the analysis of alternative marketing strategies in some detail, but is not an effective vehicle for analyzing nonmarketing strategies.

Systems dynamics   Systems dynamics, an extension of the industrial dynamics concept developed by Jay Forrester,[21] has been used in environmental assessment as well as in the more straightforward forecasting role. The discipline required in problem definition, influence diagram development, and equation structuring demands a high degree of analytical attention. Although the mathematical simulation methodology can be extended and applied to strategy evaluation and selection, the initial three steps seem to be worth the considerable testing required to determine the thoroughness or completeness of proposed alternatives. Moreover, as with any simulation model, the systems dynamics approach permits the testing of proposed strategies on a "What if?" basis. This capability, if used in the context of a structured experimental design, gives insights into the relative importance of various strategy components. For instance, an early application by Forrester demonstrated the importance of the effect of the timing of production decisions on market performance.

Metagame analysis   Game theory, as developed by T. Von Neumann and D. Morgenstern,[22] has not developed into a practical tool for assessing the impact of that most important environmental element—the competition. Metagame analysis, however, represents one innovative extension of game theory to strategy formulation.[23] This approach emphasizes the general concept of competitive equilibrium as derived from the better-known but little-used theory of games. However, because metagame analysis involves the process of mutual anticipation of competitors' strategy choices, an element that is omitted from classical game theory, and because it does not require the assumption of a simple utility function for payoff, it has greater potential applicability to business situations. Moreover, whereas game theory is primarily a strategy evaluation approach, metagame analysis is inherently part of the formulation process, since it:

1. Seeks to discover stable scenarios—those scenarios from which all competitors will find no reason to depart—and
2. Suggests to the user strategies that have been identified by the model as potentially better than the one that he or she is preliminarily considering.

Biplab Dutta and William King[24] have described an interactive computer system that integrates the complex mutual anticipation process

145

with N. Howard's metagame algorithm and mathematical market models to produce predictions of the outcomes of the complex strategy choices made by a number of competitors. This system allows strategies to be defined in terms of a number of variables, and outcomes are predicted in multidimensional form. The metagame model identifies possible sanctions that may be taken by each competitor against a proposed strategy and evaluates alternative strategies which are generated through a combinational algorithm.

The system has had only this single application in the real world of business. Despite such limited application, it appears to have potential for improving the level of sophistication of environmental analysis where it applies to the competitive environment.

Summary

This chapter presents a variety of techniques that have proved to be useful in the various phases of environmental assessment. When they are used in the context of the framework and process presented in Chapter 9, they can effectively help the firm to understand its present, its possible future, and the opportunities and problems it may face as it progresses.

Notes

1. William R. King and David I. Cleland, "Information for More Effective Strategic Planning," *Long Range Planning*, February, 1977, pp. 59–64.
2. See R. L. Ackoff, "Management Misinformation Systems," *Management Science*, December, 1967, pp. B147–B156, for a full exposition of this situation.
3. H. Kahn, and A. Weiner, *The Year 2000: A Framework for Speculation on the Next Thirty-three Years* (New York: Macmillan, 1967).
4. R. D. Zentner, "Scenarios in Forecasting," *C & E News*, October 6, 1975, pp. 23–31; and R. E. Linneman and H. E. Klein, "The Use of Multiple Scenarios by U.S. Industrial Companies," *Long Range Planning*, February, 1979, pp. 83–90.
5. Richard L. Noland and K. Eric Kuntsen, "The Computerization of the ABC Widget Company," *Datamation*, April, 1974, p. 71.
6. *Long Range Planning*, prepared by the Congressional Research Service for the Committee on Science and Technology of the U. S. House of Representatives (Washington, D.C.: U.S. Government Printing Office, May, 1976).
7. Burt Nanus, "Annual Report 1976" (Los Angeles: University of Southern California, Center for Futures Research, 1976).
8. See J. P. Martino, *Technological Forecasting for Decision Making* (New York: American Elsevier, 1972), Chapter 5.
9. For a discussion of the various econometric models that are available to subscribers, see S. Golder, "Forecast: Profits for Prophets," *New York Times*, October 19, 1975, p. F-1.
10. Delphi and the Delphi derivations used by TRW, Inc., are reported in "New Products: Setting a Timetable," *Business Week*, May 27, 1967, pp. 52–56.

11. William K. Hall, "Strategic Planning Models: Are Top Managers Really Finding Them Useful?," *Journal of Business Policy*, Winter, 1973, pp. 33–42. Brainstorming is also discussed in the context of other creativity-stimulating techniques in James L. Adams, *Conceptual Blockbusting* (San Francisco: San Francisco Book Co., 1976).

12. A. J. Rosenstein, "Quantitative—Yes Quantitative—Application for the Focus Group," American Marketing Association, *Marketing News*, May 21, 1976.

13. D. H. Meadows, D. L. Meadows, J. Randers, and W. W. Behrens, III, *The Limits to Growth: A Report for the Club of Rome's Project on the Predicament of Mankind*, (New York: Universe Books, 1972).

14. M. Mesarovic and E. Pestel, *Mankind at the Turning Point: The Second Report to the Club of Rome* (New York: E. P. Dutton, 1974).

15. M. Turoff, "The Design of Policy Delphi," *Technological Forecasting and Social Change*, vol. 2, no. 2, 1970, pp. 149–171.

16. Richard O. Mason, "A Dialectical Approach to Strategic Planning," *Management Science*, April, 1969, pp. B404–B414. An elaboration of this methodology can be found in Ian I. Mitroff and Richard O. Mason, "Structuring Ill-Structured Policy Issues: Further Explorations in a Methodology for Messy Problems," *Strategic Management Journal*, October-December, 1980, pp. 331–342. A critique of the DIS method is contained in Richard A. Crosier and John C. Aplin, "A Critical View of Dialectical Inquiry as a Tool in Strategic Planning," *Strategic Management Journal*, October-December, 1980, pp. 343–356.

17. Douglas A. Hurd and E. Riggs Monfort III, "Vulnerability Analysis," *Planning Review*, November, 1979, pp. 31–34.

18. G. W. Gershefski, "Corporate Models: The State of the Art," *Management Science*, February, 1970, pp. B303–B312.

19. T. H. Naylor and H. Schauland, "A Survey of Users of Corporate Planning Models," *Management Science*, May, 1976, pp. 927–937.

20. P. Kotler, "Corporate Models: Better Marketing Plans," *Harvard Business Review*, July-August, 1970, pp. 135–149. J. B. Boulden and E. S. Buffa, "Corporate Models: On-Line, Real-Time Systems," *Harvard Business Review*, July-August, 1970, pp. 65–83.

21. Jay W. Forrester, *Industrial Dynamics* (Cambridge: MIT Press, 1961).

22. T. Von Neumann and D. Morgenstern, *Theory of Games and Economic Behavior*, 2nd edition (Princeton, New Jersey: Princeton University Press, 1947).

23. N. Howard, *Paradoxes of Rationality: Theory of Metagames and Political Behavior* (Cambridge: MIT Press, 1971).

24. Biplab K. Dutta and William R. King, "A Competitive Scenario Modeling System," *Management Science*, March, 1980, pp. 261–274.

PART IV

STRATEGIC PLANNING
IN THE
DIVERSIFIED FIRM

CHAPTER 11

Planning in
Diversified Firms

PREVIOUS CHAPTERS have explored important internal and external aspects of the strategic planning process, with particular emphasis on organizations that have a single primary product-market relationship. In this chapter, we address the even more complex problems that confront diversified firms as they interact with multiple environmental segments and with numerous competitors.

In doing so, we shall refer back to many of the elements of the conceptual model of Chapter 2 and to some of the ideas, such as the growth-share matrix, that were introduced in the context of the overall analysis of an SBU in Chapter 3. The role of the individual SBU was introduced in Chapter 2; this chapter addresses the relative roles of many SBUs operating in concert.

The chapter discusses the diversified firm in terms of a stakeholder analysis that demonstrates the complexity involved in managing such a firm. Then, various concepts and models of a business portfolio introduce the problems of managing the diversity represented by a collection of dissimilar SBUs. The latter half of the chapter is devoted to the issues involved in strategic acquisition and divestment analysis, since acquisitions and divestments are major methods by which diversification is accomplished and by which diversified firms alter their portfolios.

Stakeholder Analysis of
the Diversified Firm

The concept of diversification has been a popular one among executives for many years, but it has led to widely varying economic results for different firms. While diversification may offer opportunities to transfer distinctive competencies or bridge market failures, it usually also inflicts the added costs of increasingly complex administration, expanded environmental surveillance, and other effects of corporate growth. Questions regarding the optimal extent of diversification are far from being resolved.[1]

Regardless of the fact that evidence about the value of diversification is mixed and sometimes conflicting, the proponents and detractors can sustain vigorous arguments because various different perspectives are available from which to argue—the positions of society, stockholders, corporate officers, division managers, and employees. Consider how a stakeholder analysis, similar to that demonstrated in Chapter 9, might reflect the different perceptions of the costs and benefits associated with diversification. As shown in Exhibit 11-1, society may view diversified firms and the strategy of diversification as mechanisms for reducing severe cyclical swings in regional labor markets. Investors, on the other hand, may feel that they have less understanding of the likely future performance of their individual securities because their investment is no longer in a particular industry, but is under the control of a group of executives who serve as investment managers.

Division managers, too, may see both potential benefits and constraints posed by the corporate diversity. Under developing or de-

EXHIBIT 11-1

Implications of Corporate Diversification

| Perspectives | Consequences | |
	Advantages	Disadvantages
Society	Shifts in labor force are modulated	Influence efforts are less direct because of corporate administrative systems and asset redeployment options
	Large-scale risk-taking ventures may be facilitated	
Stockholders	Individual security's yields are stabilized	The future of "what you own" is difficult to understand
Corporate officers	Organization's future is detached from individual products and markets	Administration is complex
Division managers	Access is provided to resources beyond usual capital market	Treatment is arbitrary, independent of performance or prospects
Employees	Cyclicality may be modulated by larger capital base	Profits may not be invested where they are earned

pressed market conditions, they may have greater access to capital than they would as separate companies; on the other hand, when they earn profits, such money may be invested in industry sectors other than their own.

As is apparent, diversified firms pose interesting opportunities and substantial challenges to a society seeking to use them as vehicles for diverse economic and social missions. The debate over benefits and appropriate controls is sure to continue, but as evidence continues to accumulate, it becomes increasingly apparent that the fruitfulness of diversification is highly dependent upon the structural characteristics of the administrative system that is used to guide the overall corporate resource allocation process.

Concepts and Models of a Business Portfolio

Recent years have witnessed the development of a variety of means of portraying business portfolios. It is useful to think of a business portfolio as analogous to a portfolio of publicly traded investment securities. Just as different securities offer various economic risks and rewards over particular time periods, so do individual operating units that function under unified control within a single corporate entity. In other words, at the corporate level executives must think in terms of a flexible collection of divisions or strategic business units that they intend to operate for varying periods of time and in ways that should continually make the package of operating units attractive as an investment unit to the financial community.

Viewed exclusively from a financial perspective, a logical planning system must seek to transfer cash flows efficiently among subunits and balance the risk-return relationships for the entire set of investments. In order to perform these functions better than they can be performed through the external capital markets, executives must make full use of internal information regarding future operations of the SBUs and be sure that investment transactions are executed as efficiently as possible. Failure to do so will eventually lead to stockholders' demands for corporate dismemberment or liquidation, as has occurred with UV Industries, SCM Corporation, Singer Corporation, and other firms.

However, most diversified firms seek to do more than simply bridge possible short-term inefficiencies in capital markets through their efforts to add value by providing improved strategies, more efficient administrative services, or substantive assistance with marketing or technological tasks.

Basic Model of a Business Portfolio

Firms that seek to develop and exercise proactive portfolio strategies reaching beyond the financial dimensions often find it helpful to conceptualize alternative product-market positions in terms of a growth-share matrix such as the one shown in Exhibit 11-2 (and discussed earlier in Chapter 3). The ultimate objective of careful positioning of SBUs in such a matrix is to stimulate consideration of strategic alternatives that are feasible for various types or classes of businesses. For example, cash cows—those businesses having a high relative market share but low growth rate—are normally expected to generate more cash flow than is required to finance their mature and profitable market position. Such excess cash flows then become available to finance the growth of star businesses or to underwrite the risks associated with aggressive development of seedling businesses.

Those developing, or seedling, businesses that successfully enhance their market positions should move into the star category and later evolve into cash cows. When failure strikes, however, the seedlings deteriorate into dogs, which then must be revitalized through improved market segmentation or liquidated through divestment or other disposal processes. The objective in all such actions, of course, is to maintain a balance of resources in the three positive cells while minimizing the problemsome businesses in the dog category.[2]

EXHIBIT 11-2

Growth-Share Matrix

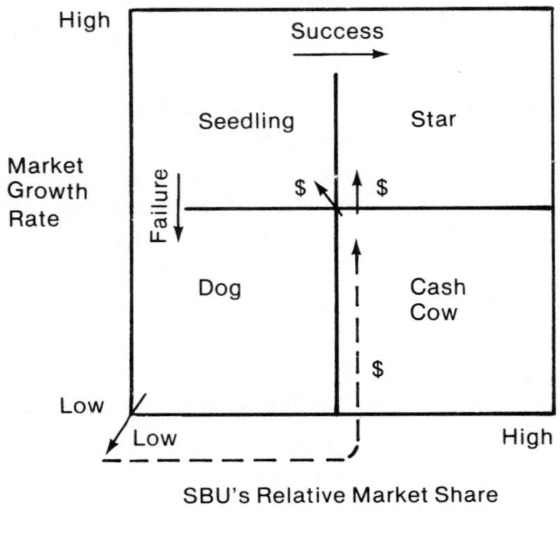

SBU's Relative Market Share

154

More Sophisticated Business Portfolio Model

The process of translating prescriptions for individual SBUs into a combination of interdependent actions throughout the portfolio requires a more complex portrayal, such as that in Exhibit 11-3. In this graphic representation, the categories of the growth-share matrix have been expanded, and eight alphabetically designated circles portraying the proportion of corporate assets devoted to each SBU have been added. Because of this portrayal, this model is sometimes referred to as a "bubble chart."

With the shaded areas indicating the estimated share of the served market that is serviced by the given SBU and the arrows indicating the strategic direction of the SBU within its market, the diagram

EXHIBIT 11-3

Balanced Diversified Portfolio
of Businesses

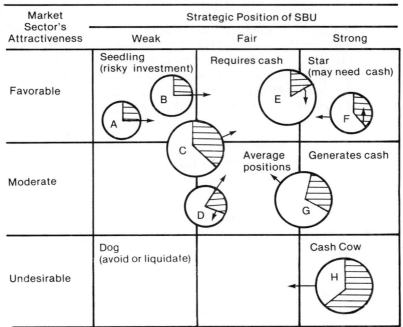

Legend:
1. The shaded area reflects estimated share of market served that is serviced by this SBU.
2. The bubble size reflects the proportion of corporate resources in the SBU.
3. The arrows indicate the direction of current SBU strategy.

155

shows both the current position and the intended future position of the portfolio components. For example, unit A is a minor investment with a 25 percent market share in a rather favorable market segment, but its position must be improved before it can become a candidate for substantial future investment. In contrast, unit F has about 40 percent of a similar market, but it is targeted to reduce its market share and relax its position in the market in order to increase margins and/or cash flow.

The dominant position of unit H is being exploited for cash and profit generation in order to support the aggressive strategies of A, B, C, and D. Unit G is seemingly prepared to sacrifice some of the strength of its current position in order to try to shift into a somewhat more attractive market segment. The potential offered by unit D must be particularly attractive, because it appears that three facets have been designated for improvement simultaneously—namely, market share, market segment, and strategic position. Thus, there is the very real possibility that the aggressive development plans of several SBUs may strain the resource generation capacity of other business units, so that some plans might have to be delayed, external resources might have to be secured, or a unit such as D might have to be sold to another corporation with the resources for rapid, broad-scale development.

The difficulty of simultaneously comprehending all the intended interrelationships among the SBUs in Exhibit 11-3 is readily apparent, and it must be remembered that many large, diversified firms have dozens of such SBUs and a few may be managing more than a hundred at a given time.[3]

Strategic Management of Business Portfolios

The strategic manager not only must comprehend the myriad interdependencies involved in the business portfolio, but must make changes in the portfolio to adjust to changing conditions and to achieve strategic objectives.

Portfolio Balance

The concept of balance is intrinsic to the strategic management of business portfolios.

Unbalanced business portfolios can develop for several different reasons, but the net result in each case is apt to be a difficult and potentially costly rebuilding period for the firm. Diversified firms with a relatively passive attitude toward markets for both products and capital may not identify enough productive investment opportunities for the cash being generated by increasingly mature businesses. The resulting cash accumulation and debt reduction can make this firm an attractive takeover target for an acquisitive firm seeking cash for expansion. For Standard Oil Company (Ohio) the challenge of excess cash arose from rapidly successful investments in Alaskan oil development rather than passive management of mature businesses, but the resulting need for an aggressive search for new investment opportunities was no less pressing.[4]

In marked contrast, a portfolio can become unbalanced as a result of the aggressive simultaneous pursuit of several high-risk seedling businesses. Without the cash and managerial resources to support such opportunities, the firm risks spreading moderate (and eventually unsuccessful) effort across a broad front or prematurely abandoning businesses with real potential. Even a firm the size of General Electric found itself with such a difficulty when it tried to pursue mainframe computers, nuclear reactors, and jet engines concurrently in the 1960s.[5] Sale of the computer business permitted support of the remaining two sectors at what was thought to be adequate levels.

A slight variation in this same form of unbalancing occurs when star businesses develop voracious cash demands as a result of a rapid spurt in the sector's growth rate or mode of operation. The resulting cash demands may be met with external financing if capital structure and financial markets permit; otherwise, divestiture may become essential to return the portfolio to approximate equilibrium. A switch from direct sales to leasing capital equipment in a growing electronics market, for example, might induce such an imbalance quite unexpectedly. A large, private holding company experienced a similar unbalancing during the 1970s when demand for coal mining equipment grew much faster than expected and forced a short-term concentration of assets in a single industry. Divestment of the large SBU followed by several small acquisitions permitted the effective rebalancing desired by the family.

A conceptual flaw in the composition or mix of SBUs can also pose serious problems of portfolio imbalance. For example, the difficulties of developing and maintaining a balanced portfolio of businesses that provide some degree of stability during cyclical swings in the general environment are well illustrated by the Trans World Corporation.[6] With the apparent intent of using cash generated by the cyclical airline industry to fund service businesses which in turn would provide a steady flow of income to absorb the substantial investment tax credits derived from intermittent major equipment purchases, Trans World acquired hotels, restaurants, vending machine operations, and

157

a real estate brokerage chain. When recessionary forces hit, however, the vending machines (which were largely in manufacturing plants) and the real estate sales operations were hurt almost as much as the airline and hotel businesses. Exacerbating the short-term realities of the downturn was the recognition that massive capital infusions would be required in both the airline and nonairline businesses if TWA was to develop a fuel-efficient fleet of planes and if the other businesses were to compete effectively with aggressive competitors.

In sharp contrast to Trans World's efforts to improve portfolio performance through further diversification, Goodyear Tire & Rubber Company has been refocusing resources in the tire segment of its businesses while many competitors claim that excess capacity in that sector will cause further market deterioration. In the context of Exhibit 11-3, we see that Goodyear's strong tire market position might serve it well regardless of the industry sector's condition; if competitors abandon a declining industry, Goodyear may be strong enough to generate strong positive cash flows. On the other hand, the General Tire and Rubber Company has decreased its portfolio commitment to the tire industry to 25 percent because it subscribes to the view that better tires, smaller cars, and higher gasoline prices will serve to shrink the market in years ahead.[7]

Portfolio deterioration can also result from the proliferation of minor market positions through internal R&D. Such "creeping capability" may initially suggest some benefits, but failure to focus marketing and manufacturing resources during individual products' growth phases can leave a firm with numerous but weak competitive positions. This phenomenon apparently developed within Union Carbide Corporation over the course of several years until it reached the point where quantum changes were required to underscore a major shift in strategic thinking.[8] By divesting or abandoning almost three dozen SBUs and product ventures, it chose to reduce its commitment to chemicals while enhancing resources in such areas as industrial gases and batteries. It is reasonable to assume, of course, that Union Carbide has more than recognized the market pressures being applied by Air Products and Chemicals, Inc.[9] against its Union Carbide's Linde Division in industrial gases and the growing interest of Gould Corporation in more sophisticated battery technology.

In these examples, we see ways in which portfolios of businesses can become unbalanced as a result of unexpected prosperity, recessionary interdependencies, and creeping capability. Although we implicitly assume that a balanced portfolio of businesses is always superior to an unbalanced one, we must recognize that the economic dynamics of continuing operations always act to disrupt any apparent short-term equilibrium. The pattern of SBU successes and failures will lead to continuing readjustment in the direction and rate of development or disinvestment in individual units.

Incremental and Quantum Portfolio Changes

It is useful to distinguish two types of portfolio changes—incremental and quantum. *Incremental* changes are those that occur on a continuous basis as the result of market interactions. *Quantum* changes are those that arise from major changes in an SBU's investment base, its portfolio role, or the acquisition or divestiture of entire subunits. Both forms simultaneously represent sources of strategic problems and means of solution.

As we consider planning options for firms' business portfolios, it is important that we recognize which of these two forms of change we are contemplating, since they imply dramatically different consequences for the firm. Before we can explore these issues in depth, however, we must review some alternative ways of managing diversity to see the implications for initiatives and controls at various levels within the organization.

Diversified Business Structures

The separation of tasks and responsibilities between corporate headquarters and the divisions may assume different forms, depending on the benefits being sought from diversification. One effective way of visualizing vertical task differentiation is to categorize tasks as in Exhibit 11-4.

Although very few firms fit perfectly within the simplified categories outlined in the exhibit, the general relationship between a large number of corporate-level functions in firms with a resource concentration in a narrow product-market sector (dominant product) and very few corporate-level functions in the financially related firms seems quite widespread. In the technically related category, the purchasing and product design responsibilities may be reversed, depending on whether the primary economic relationship is derived from efficient material use or compatible engineering designs. The most important point to note at this juncture, however, is that responsibility for capital allocation (and acquisition) and management development remains at the corporate level under the full array of divisionalized corporate forms. Therefore, as SBU sizes are determined and the mode of competition is selected, it is critical that

159

EXHIBIT 11-4

Divisional Autonomy and
Corporate Diversification

Level of Decision Control	Organizational Forms		
	Dominant Product	Technically Related	Financially Related
Corporate	Capital Allocation		
	Management Development	Capital Allocation	
		Management Development	Capital Allocation
	Purchasing		Management Development
	Product Design	Purchasing	
	Operations	Product Design	Purchasing
		Operations	Product Design
Divisional			Operations

Source: Adapted from Leonard Wrigley, "Divisional Autonomy and Diversification," unpublished dissertation, Harvard Business School, 1970.

corporate executives maintain substantive involvement and decision control if they expect the subunits to perform in a manner appropriate to their portfolio positions.

The key constraint that managers in diversified firms must recognize is that the benefits sought in economies of scale or transferable skills at the corporate level must more than offset the costs of decision-making communication required among organizational levels to gain the economic benefits. Further, determining which skills are really transferable requires more objectivity than some organizations characteristically possess.

The decision by corporate executives to participate in technically related industry segments places special demands on managers' ability to differentiate the unique aspects of each operating unit. An example of this difficulty can be found in Heublein's treatment of its Kentucky Fried Chicken (KFC) division. KFC's participation in the consumer products and leisure food market segment made it seem a logical fit for Heublein, a firm with many years of successful experience in the specialty alcoholic beverage market. However, selling a manufactured product to wholesalers is very different from selling

160

fast food to a price- and service-sensitive mobile population. Instead of recognizing the growing competitive threats from newer and more aggressive fast food chains, the company was content to install "hard-nosed, cost efficiency management techniques" which failed to effectively monitor food quality, customer service, or competitive proximity. It was not until KFC profits had plummeted to the point of visibly injuring consolidated earnings that Heublein implemented a "back-to-basics" strategy, which, ironically, had supposedly existed for many years but had simply not been implemented.[10]

Analyzing diversified business structures One means of stimulating careful analysis of the similarities and differences among separable subunits is through the preparation of a matrix such as the one in Exhibit 11-5.

Although the subunits can be arrayed in any sequence, it may be desirable to group them initially by some important variable such as manufacturing process, customer base, or economic cycle. Opportunities to exchange or coordinate such factors as technology, market intelligence, and raw material sources become apparent as such analyses are completed. Tests for logical internal consistency are possible, as in the case of regulation among the AC, DC, and DA cells.

One manager in a dynamic sector of the industrial systems market keeps a matrix consisting of dozens of memo pads behind a drawn curtain on his office wall so that opportunities to benefit from collaborative efforts among various subunits can be visualized and explored on a timely basis. Needless to say, the variables that are important enough to appear in such an analysis should also be traceable back to the strategies for the subunit in question.

Directional Policy Matrix

The expanded growth-share matrix can be extended further to provide logical directional guidance to elements through use of the directional policy matrix (DPM).[11] As shown in Exhibit 11-6, the DPM specifies generalized action patterns for SBUs depending on their matrix position as derived from industry attractiveness and competitive posture analyses. Such general actions must be tempered by a careful analysis of the distribution of competitors' positions within the industry (here plotted along the horizontal dashed line).

The illustration in Exhibit 11-6 shows that an effort by Firm 1 in Market C (C_1) to aggressively improve its strategic position might be successful if Firms 2 and 5 remain static and Firm 3 chooses to disinvest or relinquish a portion of its position. The determining

161

EXHIBIT 11-5

Interdivisional Matrix for
Comparative Evaluation of Characteristics

SBUs	A	B	C	D	E
A	////////	Raw materials	Pricing structures	Personnel needs Technical equipment	
B	Manufacturing processes	////////	Sales financing		
C	Investment intensity Regulation	Cyclicality	////////		
D	Regulation Financing needs		Regulation	////////	
E					////////

Differences

Similarities

Note: By identifying similarities among the subunits below the diagonal, the analyst can highlight opportunities for sharing skills, economies, etc. On the other hand, the differences noted above the diagonal should underscore the unique characteristics which justify the separability of the subunits.

factor may well be the relative skills and other resources that Firm 4 brings to bear in the industry as it, too, seeks to enhance its position even further. By explicitly monitoring the apparent direction of resource commitments within a given market sector over time, a firm can begin to estimate the magnitude of effort and likelihood of suc-

EXHIBIT 11-6

Directional Policy Matrix

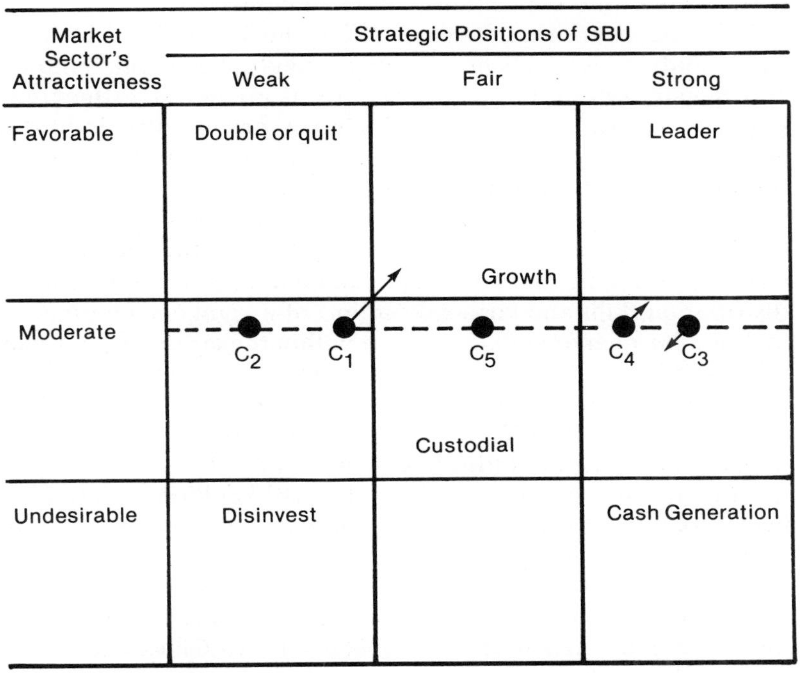

Market Sector's Attractiveness	Strategic Positions of SBU		
	Weak	Fair	Strong
Favorable	Double or quit		Leader
		Growth	
Moderate	C_2 C_1	C_5	C_4 C_3
		Custodial	
Undesirable	Disinvest		Cash Generation

Legend:
1. The arrows indicate the *direction* of a current SBU strategy; absence of arrows indicates a static posture.
2. The dashed line denotes attractiveness position of industry sector C from the perspective of company 1.
3. The numerical subscripts can refer to a separate legend of the firms that are relevant for competitive analysis in a given market.

cess to be derived from different competitors' unique sets of competitive resources.

If several major industry sectors are plotted on the same matrix, the DPM can also be valuable for assessing potential interdependencies among key rivals. It thus becomes possible to detect patterns of investment and disinvestment among several multidivisional firms simultaneously. The value of such an exercise lies in one's capacity to determine which SBUs' market positions might be vulnerable because of neglect and which firms might have difficulty in responding or retaliating because of commitments that put strong pressures on resource availability. Unfortunately, however, the logic of the analy-

163

sis of such incremental changes in competitive patterns over time can suffer major discontinuities when acquisitions or divestments alter corporations' power positions within an industry sector.

For instance, during the early 1970s, the Trojan Seed Division of Fuqua Industries was becoming increasingly successful, but the success began to strain Fuqua's cash flows as greater investments were required to support the burgeoning inventory of costly hybrid seed corn.[12] Other major hybrid seed corn producers could have reasonably inferred that Trojan's rate of expansion would be constrained within Fuqua's portfolio. However, when the decision to sell Trojan to Pfizer Incorporated was announced, the structure of competition changed dramatically, as Trojan gained access to the international distribution skills and financial support of a giant corporation.

A similar phenomenon occurred within the air deodorant market when the foundering Airwick Industries was acquired by the then cash-rich Swiss-based multinational Ciba-Geigy Corporation.[13] After a slow start in 1974–75, Ciba-Geigy's investment in new product development and marketing began to pay off as United States domestic sales of consumer products grew from $15 million to $99 million in five years, and Airwick's $2 million loss was converted to an $8 million profit on worldwide operations during the same period.[14] Needless to say, the competitive arena faced by competitors such as Clorox and S. C. Johnson & Son, Incorporated, maker of Glade deodorant, was much different from what it had been prior to Ciba-Geigy's investment in the market.

In a somewhat similar manner, the United States soft drink industry has been altered by Philip Morris's acquisition and development of 7-Up and the more recent purchase of Crush International by the Procter and Gamble Company. The competitive positions of both 7-Up and Crush, formerly comparatively weak, have been substantially reinforced by the marketing prowess and financial resources of the new parent firms. Challenges to the Coca-Cola Company's traditional market dominance have thus been coming with increased intensity, not only from Pepsico but also from sophisticated and powerful newcomers who feel they may have transferable skills and other resources of value in the market. At the same time that external domestic market pressure has been building, Coca-Cola's top management has been reorganizing with an apparent increase in attention to international markets.[15]

Simulation Analyses of Business Portfolios

The comprehension of multiple and simultaneous challenges to, and opportunities for, the strategic postures of various SBUs is ex-

164

tremely difficult without the systematic examination of a range of marketplace scenarios during the planning process. In all but the simplest situations, the development of a computer-based simulation model will be the most cost-effective means of performing such analyses.

Although simulation concepts and models have long been used at the operating and SBU levels to test functional coordination and the effects of various competitors' moves, the application of such models to corporate portfolio questions is a more recent development. In diversified corporations that integrate very little beyond cash flows, financial statements, and executive development, the simulation might incorporate relatively few variables of a largely financial nature, such as exchange rates, earnings levels, and investment cash flow estimates. However, firms that seek operating efficiencies through the sharing or exchange of numerous operating factors from raw materials to customers may require extremely sophisticated models if they hope to be able to recognize the effects of interdependencies between internal and external factors over time.

The modeling of internal corporate relationships is often difficult even if one is able to assume relative stability among external factor costs and markets, but when there are apt to be major discontinuities, such as oil embargos, new technological introductions, or major international trade agreements, the ability of modelers to anticipate the parameters is severely tested. Nonetheless, corporate simulation modeling has gained some strong supporters, and unofficial reports—such as one that Inland Steel Corporation avoided, through the use of a simulation model, a $1.5 billion investment that would have been a financial disaster—can only be expected to further stimulate development within the field.[16]

Strategic Acquisition and Divestment Analysis

The use of strategic acquisitions and divestments is an important method for implementing quantum portfolio change strategies. Such strategies are often indicated by a directional policy matrix analysis that reveals that one or more quantum changes may be necessary in order to improve long-term prospects for the firm. In such instances, acquisition and/or divestment actions may be the only way to move enough resources to new uses rapidly enough to accomplish the desired objectives.

There is evidence that this strategic view of acquisition and divestment is, in fact, currently in practice in many major business firms.[17] It seems apparent that in certain recent major acquisitions, corporate strategies have been playing a much stronger role than simply providing financial leverage. The firms that are acquired are often in relatively strong financial condition, with price-earnings multiples only slightly below those of the acquiring firms before premiums averaging almost 50 percent are added to the preacquisition market price of the sellers' common stock. In essence, economically sound companies are being acquired by other strong companies for the presumed purpose of balancing the latter's portfolio of businesses.

Similar trends in divestment behavior have been identified in research by Irene Duhaime and G. Richard Patton.[18] Their findings show that divestments are no longer just a last-ditch effort to eliminate an unsatisfying SBU, but are increasingly an integral aspect of overall management of interdependent business portfolios.

In this section we will analyze and illustrate a number of considerations that are essential to the logical use of acquisitions and divestments in the realignment of a business portfolio. The majority of our attention will be devoted to acquisition matters, because the reverse perspective will often provide guidance for divestment decisions.

Identifying Acquisition Objectives

The identification of realistic objectives for an acquisition is an essential first step if one is to successfully execute and implement the acquisition. Although the range of viable objectives is actually quite broad, managers and analysts often assume that the proper objectives are intuitively obvious and so objectives receive little attention until they surface as points of dispute during implementation. Fortunately, many such differences in perspective can be uncovered quickly and early by having each of the key decision makers assign the acquisition candidate being considered to one or two prospective positions within a business planning matrix, such as the one discussed earlier as Exhibit 11-3.

If a company to be acquired is being considered for a stand-alone role (that is, one with only financial relationships to other portfolio units) in a financially related diversified firm, objectives can quickly be narrowed to expected impacts on debt-to-equity ratios, cash flows, and earnings per share (EPS) effects. Projections regarding the future relationship with the acquiring firm can assume a high degree of operating separability along nonfinancial dimensions.

A second common acquisition objective is securing a toehold in a new and evolving market for a firm that does not have the technical

166

base or marketing network to enter the new segment efficiently on its own. Though it is a common belief that this objective is most common among opportunistic or unsophisticated firms, even a company as dedicated to internal growth through R&D as E. I. du Pont de Nemours & Company has indicated a willingness to pursue acquisitions that will provide a "toehold or springboard" for future development.[19] Prospective acquisitions to fit this objective are particularly difficult to value for bidding purposes, because substantial risks and investments will typically be required before economic returns can be expected. Companies can expect to encounter the full array of management challenges to seedling businesses, compounded frequently by lack of management familiarity with the important competitive dimensions of the embryonic market.

The enhancement of an existing product-market position is another objective that may substantially improve the strength of a strategic position or permit service to a more attractive contiguous market segment. The pursuit of this objective implies an intent to synchronize the utilization of technical, marketing, or human resources in order to gain operating efficiency or effectiveness beyond mere financial coordination. The attainment of such objectives, of course, requires more flexibility and adaptability within the firm's operation than is needed for the pursuit of either of the two prior objectives.

Another acquisition objective may be described as "defensive monitoring." Though the goal is somewhat similar to that of the toehold objective described above, the intent here is not to accelerate entry into a new market or technology but rather to remain alert to such new developments so as to minimize potential damage to an existing line of products or services. By being involved in a market in such a way, a firm can often gain access to customers' interests, labor market intelligence, and trade association activities which will provide data for assessing viable applications of the innovation being monitored. The resulting internal corporate challenge then becomes one of constructively managing the relationships between the established SBUs and the new acquisition, so that effective external monitoring can be accomplished without its resulting in harmful rivalry or internal competition.

While these objectives span a relatively broad spectrum of logical bases for acquisition activity, it must also be noted that some acquisitions may have a strong diversionary or recreational justification. Occasionally executives who no longer find existing SBUs to be exciting outlets for their entrepreneurial interests will be led to acquire businesses that simply cannot be justified in terms of portfolio balancing or any other of the above objectives, in spite of frequent efforts to

167

do so. If acquisitions made for such personal reasons can be contained at a modest scale, relatively little damage should result. Unfortunately, however, such businesses often draw much more executive attention than they deserve, because actions involving "the boss's hobby" will inevitably pique his or her interest and probable appreciation.

Criteria for Evaluation and Scope of Analysis

The acknowledgment of the objectives to be fulfilled by a particular acquisition is an important first step in this form of quantum adjustment to a business portfolio. With an understanding of the objectives to be served, the analyst is in a position to specify the criteria for evaluation and the scope of economic commitments and risks to be included in a pricing or bidding decision. For example, a prospective acquisition that is expected to serve financial objectives as an independent or stand-alone operating unit may be viewed primarily in terms of patterns of cash flows directly associated with a small number of strategic positions within an existing and well-defined market sector. A prospective acquisition that is intended to enhance the competitive position of one or more existing SBUs poses a much greater analytical challenge. Defining the nature and extent of interaction of facilities, employees, customer contacts, raw materials or components, and other factors can be a very demanding task. However, firms experiencing a significant imbalance among such functions as R&D, marketing, and production may gain substantial operating leverage from acquisitions that permit the use of idle resources or the broader exploitation of distinctive competencies.

It is essential that such criteria be formally explicated, particularly in the preliminary search phase. Publicly available information is far too vast to be of value in identifying acquisition candidates; a set of specific criteria is necessary. For instance, one company's search for acquisition candidates in the service sector quickly became bogged down in defining just what was meant by "service." The service sector of the economy is so vast that an analysis of all segments is impractical. Thus, criteria based on the objectives for the acquisition were developed. When this was done, it became apparent that many of the firms meeting the criteria were not even in the service industry (as defined by government statistics and other reports). In fact, they were manufacturing firms that provided technical service along with their manufactured products.

One frequently neglected aspect of this type of analysis is the identification of redundant resources that can be sold after the

168

acquisition is consummated. The potential disposition of duplicate resources, however, poses a particular challenge in service industries, particularly those staffed by mobile professionals. A striking example of this problem was mentioned earlier—much to the dismay of the acquiring firm, after the merger of two large brokerage firms, many of the brokers employed by the acquired firm resigned and went to work for competitors.[20] The impossibility of gaining legal title to such mobile assets means that unless acquiring firms are able to offer a substitute package of incentives that is as good as or better than available alternatives, the desired benefits may be lost and may even coalesce within a competitor's organization to the net detriment of the firm seeking to strengthen its position.

The analysis of the feasibility of acquiring particular companies as toeholds, defensive monitors, or diversionary interests primarily involves weighing the alternative costs of reaching such objectives and the probable price competing bidders are apt to pay. For example, if two or three small firms seem to have means of entering or forging dramatic new markets, such as genetic engineering, microelectronics, or solar power, the array of major bidders might push prices to extremely high levels. On the other hand, if only one or two firms have market positions worth defending through an acquisition, potential purchase prices might not reach particularly high levels. There is a growing set of analytical modes and services available to assist firms that want to evaluate numerous acquisition candidates on a very timely basis.[21]

Implementation and Assimilation of Acquisitions

Beyond defining the scope of analysis to match the portfolio objectives being sought, the manager must be certain that implementation, or assimilation, follows a course that matches the objectives. This assertion reflects the growing awareness that the actual implementation of any planned change will not necessarily occur naturally. In effect, implementation must be planned for and controlled just as is every other activity.

In implementing the assimilation of an acquisition, the first important step is the selection of reporting relationships that will permit the degree of attention or autonomy that was intended during the search and negotiation phase. A failure to establish effective communications channels at this stage may slow or alter the path of resource allocation commitments, affecting the SBU's strategic posture for years ahead.[22]

Closely related to the establishment of appropriate reporting rela-

169

tionships is the retention of intended flexibility as the acquiring firm's executives gain substantive knowledge of the firm that has just been acquired. Because it is virtually impossible to gain a comprehensive understanding of a complex operation during the typical acquisition analysis, it is important that executives strive to retain a degree of objectivity that will permit a modification of strategic objectives if new insights make such changes prudent. One example of the cost of an overly enthusiastic development agenda can be found in case of ITT's Rayonier Division. Following the acquisition of Rayonier in the late 1960s for about $300 million, ITT initiated a search for a large tract of timber that would provide a basis for its exploitation of the expectedly strong market for chemical cellulose in the years ahead. After making a preliminary commitment for a huge tract of land in Canada, the managers received evidence that future market conditions would not be as healthy as originally expected, but they apparently chose to disregard the implications of the new evidence. Before ITT finally decided to close the nearly finished plant almost a decade later, an estimated $600 million in pretax losses had been incurred.[23] Less dramatic, though nonetheless serious, problems have plagued many acquisitive firms that have been unwilling to retain essential flexibility in resource deployment after completion of an acquisition permitted more thorough analyses of actual competitive relationships within the new market environment.[24]

Developing Appropriate Performance Criteria

As important as the need to retain flexibility during the post-acquisition assimilation process is, the need to correspondingly relate the evolving acquisition objectives to the performance criteria that will be used to measure the acquisition's relative success or failure is even greater. Although the appropriateness of relating evaluation criteria to chosen portfolio objectives for a given SBU—whether internally developed or acquired—seems obvious, there are many diversified firms that implicitly use the same criteria for all SBUs, regardless of portfolio position. Not surprisingly, the SBU managers receive mixed or conflicting signals from their planning sessions and their performance reviews. The net result is a diffusion of effort and a lack of commitment to the differentiated objectives and desired rates of change within the various cells of a business planning matrix.

As a means of illustrating the possible range of useful objectives and related criteria, Exhibit 11-7 is arranged in a matrix format with the compatible indicators reflected by the cells on the diagonal. A reference to the earlier growth-share matrix cell descriptions is asso-

170

EXHIBIT 11-7

Relating Acquisition Objectives and
Performance Criteria:
An Illustration

Acquisition Objectives	Performance Criteria			
	Comparative technology	Market share	Return on investment	Cash flow
Technical development or toehold (Seedlings and stars)	Appropriate 19X0	Commitment to inefficient technology	Seldom appropriate	Seldom appropriate
Market enhancement or penetration (Stars)	May waste R&D resources	Appropriate 19X2	Jeopardizes market position	Seldom appropriate
Profit contribution from stand alone (Stars and cash cows)	Seldom appropriate	May waste advertising and promotion resources	Appropriate 19X5	Sacrifices strong market position
Cash generation (Cash cows and dogs)	Seldom appropriate	Seldom appropriate	Excess commitment to declining market	Appropriate 19X9 and forward

Note: Dates in the diagonal cells are for illustrative purposes only. An appropriate time lapse will depend on the rate of technical evolution and the marketing aggressiveness in the particular economic segment under analysis.

ciated with each objective. In recognition of the fact that few SBUs operate under a unidimensional performance objective, the exhibit indicates some of the potential risks to be monitored as combinations of criteria are used.

If this framework was being used for an acquisition executed for the purpose of market enhancement, primary evaluation attention might be directed toward the changes in the share of the desired market being served. Auxiliary or secondary objectives may be described in terms of the acquisition's impact on comparative tech-

171

nology and/or ROI shifts. In essence, the primary objective should help position a new division in the planning matrix and the secondary objectives should indicate its intended trajectory within the time frame being considered.

Despite our prescriptions for logical analyses of acquisition strategies and candidates and the foundation of research[25] that has been performed in this area of strategic management, it is wise to end with the caution that the benefits of analysis may always be limited. For example, following years of experience with acquisitions, American Can Company engaged in what they thought was a thorough analysis of a chain of retail record stores. The subsequent acquisition was followed two years later by an indictment charging that the subsidiary had engaged in the sale of counterfeit records and tapes.[26] The direct damage and cost to American Can may prove to be quite small, but the secondary consequence of damage to the retail stores' reputation in the minds of customers fearful of unwittingly getting an inferior quality counterfeit record could be much more severe.

By early 1980, Esmark Company, a multibillion-dollar firm, was considering the divestiture of its original major operating unit in order to improve performance.[27] Swift & Company, which had served as the founding unit of what was subsequently to become Esmark, had fallen victim to more efficient competitors and a huge pension liability, so Esmark announced a decision to divest both the giant Swift Division and the small but strong Vickers Energy Division. Proceeds from the expected sales would be used to repurchase 50 percent of the corporation's outstanding common stock. Apparently satisfied with the idea of Esmark's portfolio realignment, shareholders promptly bid up the firm's stock price about 60 percent in three weeks during a relatively stable stock market period. Thus, the timing and economic outcome of the strategy were somewhat foiled by outside investor forces that apparently had not been fully considered in the analysis.

Summary

This chapter extends the planning ideas of the previous chapters to incorporate the special situation of the diversified firm. The concept of a business portfolio is a central model of the diversified firm. Portfolio management, using various devices such as growth-share or directional policy matrices, permits the strategic manager to depict and understand the interrelationships among diverse business units.

Because acquisitions and divestments are important to the dynamics of a diversified firm, analyses of such decisions serve to complement portfolio models as the basic tools of strategic management in such enterprises. When such analyses are used, and when the decisions made are properly implemented, the diversified firm can be well managed despite its apparently overwhelming complexity.

Notes

1. See Stewart C. Myers, "What We Know and Don't Know About Mergers and Diversification," in A. C. Hax and Z. S. Zennatos, *The Conglomerate Firm*, Technical Report #5, Sloan School of Management, MIT, June, 1978; and Malcolm S. Salter and Wolf A. Weinhold, *Diversification through Acquisition* (New York: The Free Press, 1979) for analyses of the current knowledge of the economic results of diversification.

2. For a critique of the growth-share matrix within the context of the breakfast cereal industry, see William E. Cox, Jr., "Product Portfolio Strategy, Market Structure, and Performance" in Hans B. Thorelli, ed., *Strategy + Structure = Performance* (Bloomington: Indiana University Press, 1977).

3. "Norton Company," Intercollegiate Case Clearing House #9-377-044, is a case that describes such a complex portfolio management process in a large firm. Updated material is provided in "Norton Company: Continuing a Successful Diversification Beyond Abrasives," *Business Week*, July 9, 1979, pp. 81–82; and Robert Cushman, "Norton's Top-down, Bottom-up Planning Process," *Planning Review*, November, 1979, pp. 3–8, 48.

4. Ronald Alsop, "As Its Alaska Winnings Roll In, Sohio Studies Ways to Spend Them," *Wall Street Journal*, January 24, 1980, p. 1.

5. For a thorough analysis of General Electric's decision to relinquish the mainframe computer sector, see William E. Fruhan, Jr., *Financial Strategy* (Homewood, Illinois: R. D. Irwin, 1979), Chapter 6, "General Electric Company: Value Creation."

6. "Trans World Corporation—The Strategy Squeeze on the Airline," *Business Week*, May 19, 1980, pp. 104–107, 110, 115. Trans World's desire to gain improved economic stability through diversification is undoubtedly reflective of its recognition that the beta coefficient (a common measure of stock price's variability in relationship to overall market performance) for airlines is among the highest of major industries and that the beta coefficient for TW is near the top for the industry. For more details, see Barr Rosenberg, and James Guy, "Prediction of Beta from Investment Fundamentals," *Financial Analysts Journal*, vol. 32, no. 4, July-August, 1976, pp. 62–70.

7. "Goodyear's Solo Strategy," *Business Week*, August 28, 1978, p. 67; and "General Tire: Pondering Spinoffs to Make the Most of Its Assets," *Business Week*, September 7, 1981, pp. 98, 100, 102.

8. "Union Carbide: Its Six-business Strategy Is Light on Chemicals," *Business Week*, September 24, 1979, p. 93.

9. For more details, see "Air Products and Chemicals, Inc.," Intercollegiate Case Clearing House #9-375-370.

10. For more details, see Mitchell C. Lynch, "Gray Flannel Crowd at Heublein Bones Up on Fast Food Business," *The Wall Street Journal*, January 8,1979, pp. 1 and 21.

11. The origin of DPM is usually attributed to Shell International Chemical Company's "The Directional Planning Matrix—A New Aid to Corporate Planning," 1975, and has been expanded on in S. J. Q. Robinson, R. E. Hickens, and D. Wade, "The Directional Policy Matrix—Tool for Strategic Planning," *Long Range Planning*, June, 1978, pp. 8–16.

12. For details, see "Fuqua Industries (A)," Intercollegiate Case Clearing House #9-375-189.

13. For details, see "Ciba-Geigy Corporation (B)," Intercollegiate Case Clearing House #9-375-247.

14. "Airwick's Discovery of New Markets Pays Off," *Business Week*, June 16, 1980, pp. 139–140.

15. "Coca-Cola Executives Believe 1980 Is Critical in Battle with Pepsi," *The Wall Street Journal*, March 6, 1980, pp. 1, 18; "Gone Slightly Flat, Dr. Pepper Tries to Put Fizz Back in Its Growth," *The Wall Street Journal*, June 5, 1980, pp. 1, 18; and "Former Coke Chairman Reasserts His Power, Shaking Up the Troops," *The Wall Street Journal*, June 10, 1980, pp. 1, 23. For a description of the planning system designed to reduce the difficulties of managing growth, see "The Coca-Cola Company (B)," Intercollegiate Case Clearing House #9-370-072.

16. "Computer Games That Planners Play," *Business Week*, December 18, 1978, p. 66.

17. "Wave of Mergers Reflects Corporate Strategy More than Bargain Hunting, Analysts Find," *The Wall Street Journal*, January 31, 1978, p. 47.

18. Irene M. Duhaime and G. Richard Patton, "Sell Off," *The Wharton Magazine*, Winter, 1980, pp. 43–47. Also see "Asset Redeployment: Everything Is for Sale Now," *Business Week*, August 24, 1981, pp. 68–72, 74; and Irene Duhaime, "Influences on the Divestment Decisions of Large Diversified Firms," unpublished dissertation, Graduate School of Business, University of Pittsburgh, 1981.

19. Agis Salpukas, "Du Pont: Profits and Molecules," *The New York Times*, January 27, 1980, p. F-1; and Lee Smith, "The Making of a Megamerger," *Fortune*, September 7, 1981, pp. 58–62, 64.

20. Lee Smith, "The Mauling Merrill Lynch Never Expected," *Fortune*, October 23, 1978, pp. 78, 79, 82, 84, 88, 90.

21. See, for example, Scott A. Shay, "Setting the 'Right' Premium in an Efficient Market," *Mergers and Acquisitions*, Spring, 1981, pp. 23–28; and Richard F. McCloskey, "Software Packages for Acquisition Evaluation," *Mergers and Acquisitions*, Spring, 1981, pp. 16–22.

22. The criticality of this process is illustrated in the "CML Group," Intercollegiate Case Clearing House #9-371-426, and a related article, Charles M. Leighton and Robert Tod, "After the Acquisition: Continuing Challenge," *Harvard Business Review*, March-April, 1969, pp. 90–102. For further introduction to the growing body of literature on the implementation of decision models, management information systems, and other planned changes, see R. L. Schultz and D. P. Slevin, eds., *Implementing OR/MS* (New York: Elsevier, 1975); and W. R. King, "Implementing Strategic Plans through Strategic Program Evaluation," *OMEGA*, vol. 8, no. 2, 1980, pp. 173–181.

23. Carol J. Loomis, "How ITT Got Lost in a Big Bad Forest," *Fortune*, December 17, 1979, pp. 42–47, 50, 52, 55. A dramatically contrasting example drawn from the same industry is captured in Loren McIntyre, "Jari: A Massive Technological Transplant Takes Root in the Amazon Jungle," *National Geographic*, May, 1980, pp. 686–712. The billion-dollar gamble of Daniel K. Ludwig initially suggested a combination of detailed planning, risk taking, and good luck might revolutionize portions of the world's forest products industry. However, major difficulties developed for Ludwig, too, as documented by Gwen Kinkead in "Trouble in D. K. Ludwig's Jungle," *Fortune*, April 20, 1981, pp. 102–117.

24. The "Heublein, Incorporated (A) & (B) Condensed" case, Intercollegiate Case Clearing House #9-373-103, exemplifies the seemingly obvious synergies of moving from the distilled spirits industry into brewing via the acquisition of Hamm Brewing Company. Only the substantial losses that followed implementation proved the folly

of the easy synergy. Numerous examples are cited in Thomas Putzinger Jr., "Troubled Couplings," *Wall Street Journal*, September 1, 1981, pp. 1, 18.

25. See, for example, John P. Dory, *The Domestic Diversifying Acquisition Decision* (Ann Arbor: UMI Research Press, 1978).

26. "American Can: Diversification Brings Sobering Second Thoughts," *Business Week*, March 24, 1980 pp. 130–132. See, too, Peter Nulty, "American Can's Big Shakeout," *Fortune*, August 24, 1981, pp. 74–77, 80.

27. Meg Cox, "Esmark Is Growing Impatient with Swift as Meat Packer Remains a Drag on Profits," *The Wall Street Journal*, April 29, 1980, p. 48; Jonathan Kaufman, "Esmark Charts Reorganization of Its Structure," *The Wall Street Journal*, June 27, 1980, p. 2; and Meg Cox, "To Engineer Slick Deals, Esmark's No. 2 Man Combines Timing, Finesse, and Intimidation," *The Wall Street Journal*, June 24, 1981.

PART V

ORGANIZATIONS
AND SYSTEMS
FOR STRATEGIC PLANNING

CHAPTER 12

Organizational Structure and Processes for Strategic Management

THE EFFECTIVE STRUCTURING of organizational relationships and incentives is important for both the formulation and implementation phases of strategic planning. In this final chapter, we integrate and extend many of the concepts introduced in previous chapters. Our objective is to underscore the available evidence indicating that effective resource deployment and monitoring is highly dependent on the stimulation of creativity, the coordination of interdependent functions, and the evaluation of historical performance as an indicator of future prospects. Managers who fail to fully recognize the ways in which subordinates interpret "guidelines and feedback" cannot expect that analytical activities will be aimed in appropriate directions or that tasks will be pursued with enthusiasm.

In this chapter, we deal with the strategic restructuring of the organization itself, with the strategic assignment and development of individuals and positions within the organization, and with the strategic design of organizational systems. First, however, we review the distinctions that exist between integrated and diversified firms as they relate to the need for, and freedom of action associated with, such organizational changes.

Strategy Formulation and Implementation in Integrated and Diversified Firms

As in previous chapters, our coverage in Chapter 12 will be in terms of two major classes of firms—integrated and diversified. Exhibit 12-1 summarizes the primary distinctions between the corporate-level strategic processes in these major classes of firms.

EXHIBIT 12-1

Alternative Strategic Processes
across Classes of Firms

Strategic processes	Classes of Firms	
	Integrated	Diversified
Formulation	Single concept of firm's product-market mission derived from functional departments' interaction	Multiple concepts of firm's product-market missions derived from strength in markets and corporate portfolio positions
Implementation	Alignment of organizational structure and incentives to yield functional balance over time	Delineation of internal and external competitive requirements and innovation incentives to yield portfolio balance over time

Integrated firms must seek to develop organizational structures and administrative processes that will create a unified product-market mission consisting of balanced and mutually reinforcing functional capabilities. Excessive attention to a single function, without the maintenance of internal consistency, will usually result in economic waste and interdepartmental jealousy without economic gain. The implementation of strategy requires task specialization among departments, with information and incentive systems that foster cooperation toward a common objective. Interaction between strategy formulation and implementation is aimed at refining the efficiency with which dominant goals are pursued. There is very little incentive to stimulate competition among functional departments, because the disadvantages of potential conflict exceed the probable benefits of excelling in a single functional area.

In diversified firms, multiple concepts of product market missions are harbored under a more abstract organizational goal, usually specified in financial or economic terms. During the formulation process, there is ample opportunity to evaluate conflicting roles for the various business units within the corporate portfolio. Each proposed SBU strategy must thus satisfy the dual tests of logic—Does it promise a viable industry-sector position and does it offer a portfolio position that is consistent with those of other existing and anticipated SBUs?

Strategic implementation processes for diversified firms inevitably vary according to the degree of interrelationship desired among the SBUs. Within firms with a financial holding company orientation, vertical reporting relationships can stimulate competition among

180

SBUs with the open recognition that faltering units can be replaced through divestment and subsequent acquisitions. In contrast, firms that expect to benefit from exchange of technological data, market intelligence, or other joint resources must use a combination of criteria that will stimulate subunit excellence without detracting from cooperative behavior. The reinforcement and sanction criteria used in dealing with division managers provide strong guidance as to the desirable forms of future strategies. Hence, for diversified firms, the structural characteristics chosen for implementation inevitably set the context within which future formulation will occur.[1]

Decentralization, Divisionalization, and Diversification

Because management literature frequently uses the words diversification, divisionalization, and decentralization loosely, it is important that we define these terms.

Diversification, as we have used it, refers to the variety of product-market relationships maintained by a single firm. Thus, a firm that manufactures and sells watchbands, power saws, light aircraft, and drill presses would be characterized as being more diversified than one that produces, cans, and distributes three dozen types of vegetables.

Divisionalization here refers to a type of formal organizational structure in which various functional departments serving one specific product-market sector are clustered together in a single reporting unit which can be held accountable for its own economic performance. In other words, a division is viewed as a technically separable operating unit that would require only limited additions of legal and financial personnel in order to function independently. Although most diversified firms are also divisionalized for purposes of administrative efficiency, the same form is justified for single product firms operating in multiple locations (service stations, restaurants, cement factories, and so forth). This structure, however, does not imply any particular degree of subunit autonomy.

Decentralization describes the degree of subunit autonomy authorized by upper levels in a hierarchy. Such autonomy, or freedom of action, extends across functions and refers to the magnitude of action permitted without supervisors' authorization or consent. Because many subtle incentives and sanctions can influence the seemingly independent actions of individuals, it is extremely difficult to assess the extent of decentralization that actually exists at a given point in time.

Divisionalization does not necessarily lead directly to decentralization. This idea has been supported by Stephen Allen's research and further evidence has been advanced by Henry Mintzberg to demonstrate that single-dimension performance measures across divisions often constitute very restrictive controls.[2] Thus, there is a tendency for diversification to result in divisionalization and for it in turn to facilitate decentralization, but there is no *a priori* causal linkage between these concepts.

Strategic Structural Change

Reorganization is one of a set of management actions that can be used to maintain control over organizational resources and performance.[3] Those members of the firm with authority to implement organizational changes wield significant power, because reporting relationships, information access, and resource control determine the leverage enjoyed by participants both before and after a reorganization. Although actions to restructure an organization can have many laudable consequences in terms of improving strategic processes, it has been recognized for centuries that the converse can also result:

> We trained hard . . . but it seemed that every time we were beginning to form up into teams we would be reorganized. I was to learn later in life that we tend to meet any new situation in life by reorganizing; and a wonderful method it can be for creating the illusion of progress while producing confusion, inefficiency, and demoralization . . . .[4]

With careful planning regarding the intended consequences of reorganizations, however, confusion can be minimized and morale lifted as dedicated employees follow managers who have a new vision of the way in which a complex organization should function. When Edward Hennessy, Jr., was chosen from a list of over 100 candidates to become the new president of Allied Corporation (formerly Allied Chemical Corporation), he transferred his energies from United Technologies and quickly gained a reputation for the "cyclonic pace" with which he reallocated resources and employee efforts.[5] The reorganization of corporate and divisional activities resulted in a net reduction of 700 administrative personnel, and the investors' response was a one-third increase in per share common stock prices.

A similarly vigorous reorganization effort was implemented more than two decades ago when the lackluster performance of Crown Cork & Seal Company led John Connelly to accept organizational leadership in order to head off a threat of bankruptcy. The reconceptualization of product-market relationships and organizational discipline attributed to Connelly resulted in significant performance improvements in the following years.[6]

Textron is another example of a firm that has also begun to make significant organizational changes in order to alter the tempo of performance in its traditionally rather autonomous divisions.[7] By raising sales and profit targets, replacing some division managers, and liquidating some passive assets, the new senior executives are using a combination of "carrot" and "stick" incentives to stimulate divisional performance. One lasting result seems to be a closer monitoring of subunit activities by corporate headquarters.

Framework for Understanding Structural Change

One useful framework for understanding organizational restructuring was developed by Milton Leontiades as a result of his critiques of prior works by Scott, Wrigley, Greiner, Rumelt, Child, and others.[8] The four major stages of development shown in Exhibit 12-2 represent subdivisions of the more general integrated and diversified categories described in Exhibit 12-1. The steady-state (S) management

EXHIBIT 12-2

Matrix Model of Organizational Change:
Boise Cascade Corporation

Stage of Development	Management Mode	
	Steady-State (S)	Evolutionary (E)
Multibusiness 4. Unrelated		(1960s)
3. Related		
Single Business 2. Dominant	(1978)	(1973)
1. Single	(1931) (1950s)	

Source: Adapted from Leontiades, Milton, *Strategies for Diversification and Change*, pp. 74 and 75, Copyright ©1980 by Milton Leontiades. Reprinted by permission of the publisher, Little, Brown and Company.

183

mode represents a static period during which there is no significant change in organizational structures or processes. In contrast, the evolutionary (E) mode characterizes the turbulent transition from one structure to another. The use of this model is depicted in Exhibit 12-2 with reference to the Boise Cascade Corporation.

Following its formation in 1931, Boise Cascade spent more than two decades developing its lumber business through vertical integration. During the 1960s, however, there was a horizontal shift into an evolutionary mode and a radical vertical shift toward acquisitions of unrelated businesses ranging from plastics to recreational vehicles and computer services. Difficulties with the simultaneous management of numerous unrelated businesses led to a program of retrenchment and divestment of more than a dozen operating units in the early 1970s. Thus, by 1978 its evolutionary activities were largely completed, and Boise Cascade had returned to a steady-state mode, with its dominant resource commitment once again in the forest products industry.

ITT has also experienced a somewhat similar proactive acquisition pattern followed by a divestment and retrenchment phase. During 1979 and 1980, this giant unrelated-product firm closed or sold more than thirty business units with combined annual sales in excess of $1 billion per year.[9]

The restructuring of an organization can be a difficult process in a firm with a common "administrative inheritance" built on years of working relationships, but the challenges of change can be even greater when corporations are merged or new subsidiaries are acquired. As Kennecott's President Wendel was quoted as saying after the firm's acquisition of Carborundum, "Integrating the managements of these two companies is like merging two different cultures."[10]

Diagnosing the Need for Reorganization

In order to decide on an appropriate means of intervention for improving subunit performance, managers must distinguish between situations involving operating inefficiencies and those involving improper strategic positioning.[11] Once different sources of stagnation have been diagnosed, managers are able to choose an appropriate set of remedies for overcoming the stagnation or deterioration in subunit performance.[12] After an analysis of an SBU's economic position and the possible causes of the weak position has been completed, the manager's challenge is to select a process for taking corrective action without destroying the strengths of existing administrative procedures.

184

Corporate-level intervention in deteriorating divisional performance is particularly difficult, because basic decentralization concepts
must often be violated in order for an understanding of underlying
causes to be established. In other words, executives must balance the
need for current analytical detachment and objectivity against the
usual background of prior support and commitment.[13] The problem
is difficult for both the division manager and the corporate executive,
because their understandings of shared risk taking and assignment of
responsibility for the current crises are usually somewhat ambiguous.
Nonetheless, the intervention must distinguish between strategic and
operating shortcomings and those involving controllable versus uncontrollable factors. Some examples of the situations giving rise to the
need for various forms of intervention can be seen in Exhibit 12-3.

The division manager of a mature product line, for example, might
face any of several causes of substandard performance that would
demand interpretation and action by a senior corporate officer. A
strategic crisis from a controllable cause is readily apparent in the
case of a manager who consistently downgrades R&D and marketing
research activities until competitors are able to eventually dominate
his or her technical position. Under such circumstances, the division
manager must be able to demonstrate that senior executives had
deliberately chosen to milk the division if he or she is to escape
responsibility.

On the other hand, if the loss of a division's technical strength can
be attributed to a radical breakthrough by a substitutable technology
(integrated circuits to replace transistors, for example), which the
corporate-level executives chose not to monitor and/or develop, then
responsibility for the division's demise is appropriately attributed to
the senior executives.

Operating crises can also arise from factors either within or beyond
a division manager's effective control. As suggested in Exhibit 12-3, if
a manufacturing plant's renovations or new pieces of equipment are
installed carelessly so as to detract from efficient operations, the
responsibility inevitably lies with the division manager and division
staff. In contrast, deteriorating margins that result from industrywide
regulatory changes regarding pollution abatement or employee
benefits can hardly be described as the exclusive responsibility of the
current operating manager.

Although we have sought to demonstrate the usefulness of the
diagnostic framework for assigning responsibility for declining subunit performance with relatively simple and clear-cut examples,
many actual situations represent combinations of these causes that
accrue over several measurement periods. Making a distinction between a series of operating factors and a single strategic cause can

185

EXHIBIT 12-3

Diagnostic Framework for
Subunit Performance Difficulties

Extent of control	Source of crisis	
	Strategic	Operating
Controllable	Weak technical position in evolving market	Inefficient operations from poor plant layout and lax controls
Uncontrollable	Loss of market to technical breakthrough in related technology	New and costly government regulations or industry-wide labor settlement

then be quite difficult. Similarly, with changing hierarchical relationships, it may be very difficult to determine who actually chose to minimize a division's R&D if a firm's quest for annual profit improvements was very intense. Careful documentation of alternatives and trade-offs that have been considered is usually the best way to help ensure that subsequent interpretation of results will capture the causal factors that were analyzed and the choices that were made. Without such records responsibility may shift because of new participants and perspectives, selective memory regarding situations and decisions, or reliance on traditional procedures for interpreting performance variances.

Assignment and Development of Management

Division of authority is most often thought of as an element of management, but not necessarily of *strategic* management. Nonetheless, in times of stress, such as those in which reorganizations are under consideration or are underway, the assignment of specific tasks to the right people can be of critical importance. Moreover, the development and assignment of individuals to specific positions in a complex firm is indeed a continuing strategic concern.

Assignment of Strategic Tasks

Regardless of whether one's reorganization framework is for a long-established corporation or a recently formed firm, it is important that distinctions be made among tasks in terms of their criticality and urgency before they are assigned to various managers. As used in the

186

framework of Exhibit 12-4, criticality refers to the strategic importance attached to an individual decision or a class of decisions. Urgency refers to the speed or quickness with which action must be
taken. In Exhibit 12-4, the chief executive officer (CEO) is to reserve
the majority of his or her time for activities of critical importance to
the organization, some of which inevitably will also be urgent. The
president or chief operating officer (COO) would typically assume
responsibility for more of the urgent actions, particularly those with
less than utmost criticality. Division and/or functional line managers
would then be responsible for all urgent decisions of lesser criticality.
As the degree of task urgency is reduced, senior-level and staff personnel become responsible.

The objective of defining areas of managerial responsibility and
positioning activities on a matrix such as Exhibit 12-4 is to provide a
basis for shared understanding of which positions should be primarily
concerned with which types of work. For example, the manufacture
and sale of existing product lines requires the attention of numerous
line managers if goods are to be converted and delivered efficiently.
On the other hand, the analysis of new product entries, divestment
options, and evolving government regulations may be as critical, but
somewhat less urgent.

As particular issues move from a state of preliminary exploration
and analysis to implementation, they will typically increase their

EXHIBIT 12-4

Management Activity Analysis of Critical
versus Urgent Issues: An Illustration

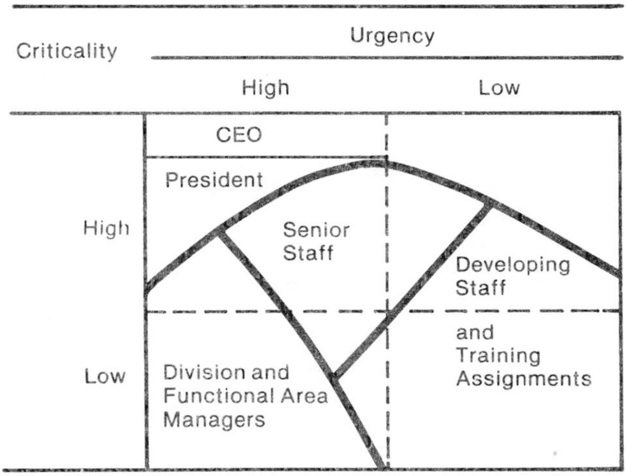

187

degree of urgency, but the level of criticality may either increase or decline.

Assignment of Managerial Positions

Management selection and training systems are important in diversified firms because various types of people must be encouraged to pursue different objectives simultaneously.[14] Analyses by Derek Channon have led him to view division managers' tasks in terms of their positions within a given portfolio. Given the broad spectrum of demands that can be placed on general managers responsible for SBUs in different portfolio positions, it is increasingly recognized that all such individuals are not equally qualified to manage all types of businesses.

Exhibit 12-5 shows, for example, that an SBU seeking market growth from the position of a seedling would probably benefit most from leadership by an entrepreneurial person who has a future orientation and is willing to seek change, even if it means accepting risk. On the other extreme, the person responsible for a cash cow SBU should be willing to stress consistent current performance and the avoidance of risk. The manager of a star business in search of profitability must carefully but aggressively pursue a balanced perspective in order to stay abreast of expanding opportunities without risking an established market position.

It is therefore essential that efforts be made in personnel selection and development and in incentive system design to foster the combination of skills and motivations required to conquer such divergent tasks. General Electric[15] and other firms have reportedly begun mold-

EXHIBIT 12-5

Management Characteristics for
Different Business Portfolio Positions

Management characteristics	Portfolio position objectives		
	Market growth	Profitability	Cash flow
Style	Entrepreneurial	Careful	Efficiency seeking
Perspective	Future development	Balanced progress	Current performance
Flexibility	Seeks change	Accepts variety	Avoids change
Orientation	Risk taker	Neutral on risk	Risk avoider

Source: Derek F. Channon, "Commentary" on J. H. Grant and W. R. King, "Strategy Formulation: Analytical and Normative Models," in D. E. Schendel and Charles W. Hofer, eds., *Strategic Management: A New View of Business Policy and Planning* (Boston: Little, Brown, 1979), p. 132.

ing managerial job environments to meet the specialized demands of particular business portfolio positions, but such efforts to customize the fit between general management tasks and structural variables remain the exception rather than the rule in business practice.

In spite of the critical importance of the overall human resource planning function within firms seeking continuity in strategic processes, there is ample evidence to suggest that it remains an underdeveloped function in most organizations.[16] Planning, however, can serve as a catalyst for enhancing the sophistication of the human resource development function.[17] Logical strategic planning activities demand both a sophisticated managerial perspective and a thorough set of analytical abilities, so the selection, assignment, and training of personnel in this area become critical. The converse, of course, also applies; as executives become more capable and confident, they are able to conceptualize and implement more effective strategies.

Designing Organizational Systems

In addition to providing for organizational restructuring and the assignment and development of key managers, organizational systems can be used as instruments of strategic change in business firms. These systems may focus on motivating managers to seek creative solutions that are appropriate for the strategy by which the firm is seeking to influence its future. Alternatively, the planning system itself can provide mechanisms for achieving desired change.

Implementing Motivational Systems

The successful execution of desired strategies requires that managers be motivated in ways that are consistent with the strategies. It does little good to tell a manager to follow a particular strategy if he or she is being motivated by salary, bonuses, and other devices to follow a different strategy. According to one of its executives, a large chemical firm abandoned its complex performance incentive program and returned to annual cash bonuses for high achievers when it realized that managers were receiving "a garbled message as far as what performance really meant. They would have four different goals for the same year."[18]

Performance appraisal is an area that demands careful attention if formal systems are to receive the managerial support needed for their successful implementation. This process, however, remains among the thorniest facing managers, as they must develop systems that are systematic enough to meet legal requirements, yet simple and per-

189

sonal enough to be understood by the employees and their supervisors.[19] Complexity arises from the need for general managers to perform satisfactorily across several functional dimensions while maintaining a balanced time perspective.

The difficulty of effectively linking major corporate resource commitments with long-term expected benefits to the incentive system is exacerbated in organizational structures with numerous hierarchical levels.[20] In order to get ahead in career terms, most managers feel a strong urge to frequently seek better jobs. The net result is that the originators of strategic proposals are often not available for the crucial implementation process, and they are even less apt to be in a position to assume responsibility for the projected performance once the full scale operation is achieved. Some scholars have recommended that in order to minimize this problem managers should remain in particular assignments for a greater number of years, and successful ones should then be rewarded with multilevel promotions of greater significance.[21] The intent of such proposals is to ensure that managers have a few complete cycles of experiences proposing, implementing, and having evaluated their strategic moves before they reach the most senior positions in a firm.

Although many companies continue to be critized for overemphasizing short-term performance criteria in their incentive compensation systems, there is an increasing trend toward linking top executives' financial rewards to longer-term measures.[22] Honeywell, for example, reportedly rewards its forty top executives according to growth in annual earnings per share, and Champion International bases its pay-outs on the firm's performance relative to fifteen competitors within the forest-products industry.

Within diversified firms, the motivation of managers is influenced by the persistent tension between the possible benefits to be derived from collaborative or synergistic relationships among technically or market-related units and the alternative gains that might arise from innovative behavior that is stimulated by competition. These opposing forces are both attractive and are thus sought simultaneously by many large firms, so there is little surprise that communication essential to stimulating desired behavior is often misdirected or misinterpreted.

Effective communication within large organizations is always difficult, but when those structures are also diverse and dynamic, the problems of adequate and timely communication are even more difficult. Under such circumstance, "perceptions become the truth."[23] Perceptions, of course, constitute the context within which data are processed and conclusions are drawn. In the minds of senior executives, for example, enthusiastic behavior of subordinates may be viewed as commitment when in fact it merely reflects compliance.[24] On the other hand, employees may view the meteoric rise of one of their peers as favoritism because they cannot accept the fact that it might reflect superior performance, a promotion criterion they themselves have long espoused. Thus, when a bright, young, female MBA progressed rapidly through the ranks at Bendix under the mentorship of the young male CEO, it should not have been surprising that rumors of preferential treatment would abound throughout the executive corridors.[25] Reliable communication of expectations is especially difficult in diversified organizations that seek cooperative behavior in some spheres while simultaneously stimulating competition in others. Under such circumstances, incentive systems play a vital role in signaling appropriate behavior.

Measurements and incentives Special care must be given to the identification of evaluation criteria and the awarding of recognition in complex organizations if notions of equity and goal congruence are to be reinforced. Many large corporations continue to place primary reliance on historical financial results measured over a single year as a basis for raises, promotions, bonus payments, and other rewards. Such preoccupation with unidimensional measures presumes a degree of product maturity and competitive stability that is unrealistic for many market segments. Those divisionalized firms that operate relatively homogeneous subunits such as restaurants, apartments, and service stations may find that similar short-term financial criteria serve them quite well. Unfortunately, however, firms that use such measures while working with a diverse portfolio will find themselves stymieing innovations and overinvesting in declining businesses.

As a means of recognizing the importance of rapidly changing financing or capital costs in the evaluation of subunit performance, some firms have begun to experiment with a measure of Return After Capital Charge (RACC). The RACC percentage is calculated by subtracting the estimated average corporate cost of capital from the ROI. Clearly, the objective of such a measure is to facilitate comparisons among businesses of varying size and character. However, such a criterion offers the potential for misleading comparisons if varying financing costs are not recognized. If the cost of capital is individually estimated for different classes of SBUs within a firm's portfolio, the analyst can begin to determine rather quickly which businesses show promise of generating returns commensurate with their expected risks.

In order to stimulate divisional managers' attention to performance dimensions that are consistent with the subunit's portfolio position, it becomes necessary to move beyond a single ROI or other criterion. Companies that have encouraged corporate executives to focus on technological advances, market positions, and management development in addition to current profits are better able to recognize and implement new, innovative market initiatives.[26]

The Norton Company is one large diversfied firm that has made a significant effort to accommodate diversity in its reward structure.[27] By developing dozens of sets of performance criteria for its numerous SBUs, it has attempted to customize goals for its division managers while implicitly shifting the difficulties of complex performance interpretation and appraisal to the corporate-level executives. A strong objective of this system is to stimulate innovative behavior while also taking full advantage of mature products' positions.

Design of Strategic Planning Systems

As a result of measurement systems that are overly narrow and rigid, many organizations have a tendency to become homogeneous subcultures in which it is very difficult to thoroughly explore or test alternative strategic positions or options. Although the planning system may itself be structured in such a way as to do this, more frequently neglect or carelessness is the cause. One of the ways in which a planning system can itself influence strategic change is through the pressures that it puts on people to be creative, to consider alternatives, and to conduct thorough analyses.

For instance, the "multiple scenario planning" structure developed by Shell[28] has gained a reputation for being effective at introducing heretical views because scenarios are usually presented in starkly contrasting pairs, thus forcing thorough examination of underlying assumptions and causal relationships. Such an approach seems to be an effective application of the dialectical procedures proposed by Richard Mason for examining distinct alternatives.[29] The exploration of new ways of viewing or thinking about strategic issues is only part of the challenge; success depends on effective mechanisms for implementing revised views.

Based on his planning experiences with both General Electric and Gillette, John Bush suggests there are five key elements required of a planning system designed to stimulate internal growth:[30]

1. Ability to coordinate diverse units through some matrix structure.
2. Designation of project teams to focus on innovative ideas.
3. Environments that facilitate communication and the movement of people.

4. Linkage of profit and loss responsibility to a line organization during commercialization.
5. Measurement and reward systems that balance time perspectives.

There is increasing evidence that not only the existence of formal supporting mechanisms but also the systematic timing of initiatives are critical to the development of organizational support for significant changes in procedures or resource deployment.[31] James Brian Quinn has called such a sequence of interrelated analyses and decisions "logical incrementalism."[32] Under such an open-system management mode, there is an explicit effort to provide organizational direction without making formal commitments to specific means of accomplishment. Hence, organizational members are urged to seek the best methods of accomplishing various tasks at the time at which they must be achieved. This process legitimizes continuous search for innovative problem solutions, and it encourages adaptive responses to observable competitive behavior. The challenge, of course, is to maintain an adequate emphasis on task completion to ensure that the paralysis of analysis does not undermine timely progress.

Planning systems development   The successful implementation of a logic-based strategic plan will not occur if explicit attention is not directed toward the systematic incorporation of organizational goals, relationships, information sources, and incentives into a strategic planning system. However, such systems serve many purposes and are thus time-consuming and costly to implement. Therefore, it behooves the skillful executive to develop a "plan for planning" that will guide the development and refinement of complementary elements over time.[33] For example, it is usually inappropriate to devote significant resources to detailed competitive analyses for all elements of a corporate portfolio until a preliminary assessment has determined that each SBU is pursuing an individually logical strategy. In other words, it is important that the analytical procedures and organizational structural elements be initiated and refined at similar levels of sophistication, so participants will see interrelationships easily and recognize the credibility of that which is being pursued.

Separating strategic and operational plans   Effective positive change will occur in an organization only if "the short run is not permitted to drive out the long run." This means that an important aspect of effective strategic planning system design involves the application of criteria for distinguishing an organization's strategic plans from its operating ones.
One way of doing this is illustrated by Texas Instruments's OST

system. The OST (objectives, strategies, and tactics) system is an example of a refined set of planning elements that seek to stimulate innovation and pursue operating efficiency at the same time.[34] By separating the annual routine division-level operating activities from the corporate-level strategic (OST) activities, the corporation is able to press for current operating efficiency without risking the sacrifice of investment in future-oriented developmental work. At the same time, there is an explicit effort to educate a broad spectrum of the managerial cadre about both the spirit and the procedures surrounding the OST system. In fact, some have described the TI executives in Dallas as possessing "a Japanese-style culture under a ten-gallon hat."

While TI's OST system distinguishes between operating and strategic responsibility in terms of vertical organizational relationships, further distinctions must also be made in terms of types of objectives and time horizons. John Camillus and John Grant have developed such a framework, and an example is presented in Exhibit 12-6. The primary emphasis in these two interdependent planning processes is on eliminating the prevailing fixation with annual planning routines

EXHIBIT 12-6

Two-cycle Process for
Integrating Levels of Planning

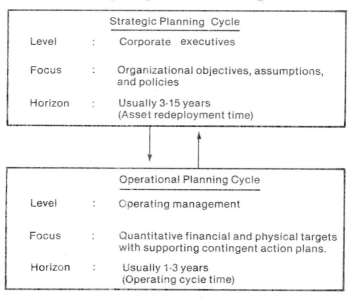

Strategic Planning Cycle		
Level	:	Corporate executives
Focus	:	Organizational objectives, assumptions, and policies
Horizon	:	Usually 3-15 years (Asset redeployment time)

Operational Planning Cycle		
Level	:	Operating management
Focus	:	Quantitative financial and physical targets with supporting contingent action plans.
Horizon	:	Usually 1-3 years (Operating cycle time)

Source: Adapted from John C. Camillus and John H. Grant, "Operational Planning: The Integration of Programming and Budgeting," *Academy of Management Review*, July, 1980, pp. 369–379.

194

which seems to dominate the planning systems and procedures in most organizations.

Under the two-cycle process, the operations plans would span the time required to execute an operating cycle within a given industry. Such cycles might be weekly in a bakery, quarterly in a department store, biannual in residential construction, and so forth. The strategic cycle, on the other hand, extends beyond the operating cycle to a point at which significant asset redeployment could occur. By thus distinguishing the appropriate frequency of planning cycle repetition, the strategist is able to be sure that thorough coverage is provided without unnecessary expense or boredom. Further justifications for reducing the importance of annual planning cycles in organizations lie in the difficulties of matching individuals' skills, organizational levels, and essential planning-structure relationships on a routine basis.[35]

Summary

This chapter extends the notion of strategy beyond the usual business context to consider the potential for strategic change in terms of organizational structure, the strategic assignment and development of individuals, and the design of organizational systems. All of these activities are important devices for ensuring the successful implementation of strategies.

This book thus ends on a note similar to that on which it began—that while the logic of strategic planning is important, it is not the sole dimension by which planning should be gauged. Strategic change in organizations occurs through the efforts of people, and although change may be guided by such strategic actions as reorganization, personnel assignments, and systems development, the ultimate potential and responsibility for strategic change rests within the managers themselves.

Notes

1. David I. Hall and Maurice A. Saias, "Strategy Follows Structure!" *Strategic Management Journal*, April-June, 1980, pp. 149–163.

2. Stephen A. Allen, "Organizational Choices and General Management Influence in Divisionalized Companies," *Academy of Management Journal*, September, 1978; and Henry Mintzberg, *The Structuring of Organizations: A Synthesis of the Research* (Englewood Cliffs, New Jersey: Prentice-Hall, 1979).

3. Stephen A. Allen, "Understanding Reorganizations of Divisionalized Companies," *Academy of Management Journal*, December, 1979, pp. 641–671.

4. Attributed to Gaius Petronius, a Roman satirist of the first century A.D.

5. Peter W. Bernstein, "The Hennessy Hurricane Whips Through Allied Chemical," *Fortune*, December 17, 1979, pp. 98–101.

6. "Crown Cork and Seal," Intercollegiate Case Clearing House #6-373-077.

7. "Textron: Shaking Up the Divisions to Enliven a Sluggish Conglomerate," *Business Week*, May 26, 1980, p. 88.

8. See Milton Leontiades, *Strategies for Diversification and Change* (Boston: Little, Brown, 1980), Chapter 4, "The Matrix Model: A Synthesis of the Change Process."

9. "ITT: Groping for a New Strategy," *Business Week*, December 15, 1980, p. 66.

10. "Why Carborundum Is Changing Kennecott," *Business Week*, August 7, 1978, p. 57. The pervasive importance of organizational culture is reflected in "Corporate Cultures: The Hard-to-Change Values That Spell Success or Failure," *Business Week*, October 27, 1980, p. 148.

11. Dan E. Schendel, G. Richard Patton, and James Riggs, "Corporate Turnaround Strategies: A Study of Profit Decline and Recovery," *Journal of General Management*, Spring, 1976, pp. 3–11.

12. Charles W. Hofer, "Turnaround Strategies," *Journal of Business Strategy*, Summer, 1980, pp. 19–31.

13. Richard G. Hamermesh, "Responding to Divisional Profit Crises," *Harvard Business Review*, March-April, 1977, pp. 124–130.

14. "Wanted: A Manager to Fit Each Strategy," *Business Week*, February 25, 1980, p. 166.

15. Michael G. Allen, "Strategic Problems Facing Today's Corporate Planner," speech to the Academy of Management, Kansas City, August, 1976.

16. James A. Craft, "Human Resource Planning: An Emerging Dimension of Management," *Managing*, no. 3, 1979, pp. 5, 32.

17. Deborah J. Cornwall, "Human Resource Programs: Blue Sky or Operating Priority?" *Business Horizons*, April, 1980, pp. 49–55.

18. John Curley, "More Executive Bonus Plans Tied to Company Earnings, Sales Goals," *The Wall Street Journal*, November 20, 1980, p. 29.

19. "Appraising the Performance Appraisal," *Business Week*, May 19, 1980.

20. "Managers Who Are No Longer Entrepreneurs," *Business Week*, June 30, 1980, p. 81.

21. Joseph L. Bower, *Managing the Resource Allocation Decision* (Boston: Harvard Business School, 1970).

22. John Curley, "More Executive Bonus Plans Tied to Company Earnings, Sales Goals," *The Wall Street Journal*, November 20, 1980, p. 29.

23. From remarks by Richard J. Farris, Chairman of the Board, United Airlines, in an address at the "Leadership and Education for Leadership" conference at the University of Pittsburgh, May 22, 1979.

24. Abraham Zaleznik, "Power and Politics in Organizational Life," *Harvard Business Review*, May-June, 1970, pp. 47–60.

25. Peter W. Bernstein, "Upheaval at Bendix," *Fortune*, November 3, 1980, pp. 48–56.

26. Frederick W. Gluck et al., "Cure for Strategic Malnutrition," *Harvard Business Review*, November-December, 1976, pp. 154–165.

27. For background on the company, see "Norton Company," ICCH #9-377-044; more recent published material can be found in "Norton Company: Continuing a Successful Diversification Beyond Abrasives," *Business Week*, July 9, 1979, p. 81, and Robert Cushman's "Norton's Top-down, Bottom-up Planning Process," *Planning Review*, November, 1979, pp. 3–11.

28. "Shell's 'Multiple Scenario Planning': A Realistic Alternative to the Crystal Ball," *World Business Weekly*, April 7, 1980, pp. 14–15.

29. Richard O. Mason, "A Dialectical Approach to Strategic Planning," *Management Science*, April, 1969, pp. B403–B414. Also see Ian I. Mitroff and James R. Emshoff, "On Strategic Assumption-Making: A Dialectical Approach to Policy and Planning," *The Academy of Management Review*, January, 1979, pp. 1–12.

30. John B. Bush, Jr., "Major Growth through Internal Development," *Planning Review*, November, 1980, pp. 28–34.

31. James Brian Quinn, "Managing Strategic Change," *Sloan Management Review*, Summer, 1980, pp. 3–20.

32. James Brian Quinn, *Strategies for Change: Logical Incrementalism* (Homewood, Illinois: R. D. Irwin, 1980).

33. For a thorough treatment of this process, see W. R. King and D. I. Cleland, *Strategic Planning and Policy* (New York: Van Nostrand Reinhold, 1978), Chapter 2, "Strategic Planning Systems"; or Peter Lorange, *Corporate Planning: An Executive Viewpoint* (Englewood Cliffs, New Jersey: Prentice-Hall, Inc., 1980).

34. For a thorough description of the system, see "Texas Instruments Incorporated: Management Systems," Intercollegiate Case Clearing House #9-172-054; and "Texas Instruments Shows U.S. Business How to Survive in the 1980s," *Business Week*, September 18, 1978, pp. 66–76.

35. For a further analysis of these issues, see Milton Leontiades, *Strategies for Diversification* (Boston: Little, Brown, 1980), Chapter 5.

AUTHOR INDEX

Abernathy, William J., 84n, 97n
Ackerman, Robert W., 35n
Ackoff, Russell L., 123, 131n, 146n
Adams, James L., 147n
Aguilar, Francis J., 131n
Allen, Michael G., 196n
Allen, Stephen A., 182, 195n
Amariuta, Ion, 131n
Anderson, Carl R., 72n
Ansoff, H. Igor, 97n
Aplin, John C., 147n
Aristotle, 95, 97n

Biggadike, Ralph, 101, 107n
Boulder, J. B., 144, 147n
Bower, Joseph L., 196n
Buffa, E. S., 144, 147n
Bush, John B., Jr., 197n
Buzzell, Robert D., 83n, 107n

Camillus, John C., 194
Castleman, Breaux B., 84n
Caves, R. E., 50n
Channon, Derek F., 188
Christensen, H. Kurt, 97n
Cleland, David I., 50n, 70, 119, 121,
    124, 133, 197n
Cooper, Arnold C., 101, 107n
Cornwall, Deborah J., 196n
Cox, William E., Jr., 173n
Craft, James A., 96, 98n, 196n

Crosier, Richard A., 147n

Day, George S., 72n
Dhalla, N. K., 70, 72n
Dory, John P., 175n
Drucker, Peter F., 61n
Duhaime, Irene M., 166, 174n
Dutta, Biplab K., 146, 147n

Emshoff, James R., 197n

Fahey, Liam, 127, 128, 131n
Farris, Richard J., 196n
Forbis, John L., 97n
Forrester, Jay W., 145, 147n
Foster, Richard N., 97n
Fox, H., 68, 72n
Fruhan, William E., Jr., 61n, 97n,
    173n

Galbraith, Jay R., 19n
Gale, Bradley T., 83n,107n
Gershefski, G. W., 143, 147n
Gilmour, Peter, 84n
Gluck, Fredrick W., 97n, 196n
Graham, Kenneth R., 14n
Graham, M. B. W., 97n
Grant, John H., 97n, 194
Guy, James, 173n

Hall, David I., 195n

199

Hall, Robert W., 84n
Hall, William K., 142, 147n
Hamermesh, Richard G., 196n
Harrigan, Kathryn R., 72n, 84n
Hax, Arnaldo C., 173n
Hayes, Robert H., 103, 104, 107n
Heskett, James L., 72n
Hirschmann, W. B., 83n
Hofer, Charles W., 68, 72n, 196n
Howard, N., 146, 147n
Hunt, Michael S., 84n
Hunt, Pearson, 61n
Hurd, Douglas A., 143, 144, 147n

Jackson, Barbara, 65, 72n
Jerrell, S. Lee, 34n

Kahn, Herman, 136, 146n
Keegan, Warren J., 131n
Kefalas, Asterios, 131n
Kennedy, Ronald D., 131n
King, William R., 50n, 70, 88, 89, 97n,
    119, 121, 124, 127, 131n, 146,
    147n, 174n, 197n
Klein, Harold E., 131n, 146n
Knutsen, K. Eric, 146n
Kotler, Philip, 144, 147n

Leighton, Charles M., 174n
Leone, Robert A., 130n
Leontiades, Milton, 183, 196n, 197n
Levitt, Theodore, 6, 14n, 72n
Linneman, R. E., 146n
Lorange, Peter, 197n
Lubar, Robert, 84n

Martino, J. P., 146n
Mason, Richard O., 143, 147n, 196n
McCloskey, Richard F., 174n
Meadows, Dennis, 142, 147n
Meitz, A. A., 84n
Mesarovic, M., 147n
Michael, G., 70, 72n
Miller, Jeffrey G., 84n
Mills, D. Quinn, 97n
Mintzberg, Henry, 182, 195n
Mitroff, Ian I., 147n, 196n
Monfort, E. Riggs, III, 143, 144, 147n

Montgomery, David B., 131n
Morgenstern, D., 145
Murray, Edwin A., Jr., 124, 131n
Myers, Stewart C., 173n

Nanus, Burt, 146n
Nathanson, Daniel A., 19n
Naylor, Thomas H., 107n, 147n
Noland, Richard L., 146n

Patton, G. Richard, 15n, 166, 174n,
    196n
Peters, Ann H., 131n
Porter, Michael E., 50n, 78, 84n, 130n

Rao, Ram C., 84n
Rappaport, Alfred, 61n
Regenstrief, Samuel, 84n
Richards, Max D., 14n
Riggs, James, 196n
Rink, David, 68, 72n
Robinson, S. J. Q., 173n
Rosenberg, Barr, 173n
Rosenblum, John W., 118, 131n
Rosenstein, A. J., 147n
Rothschild, W. E., 50n
Rumelt, Richard P., 14n, 35n, 78, 84n,
    107n
Rutenberg, David P., 84n, 131n

Saias, Maurice A., 195n
Salter, Malcolm S., 15n, 173n
Schauland, H., 147n
Schendel, Dan E., 15n, 196n
Schoderbek, Peter P., 131n
Schultz, R. L., 174n
Scott, Bruce R., 19n, 131n
Shapiro, Benson, 65, 72n
Shay, Scott A., 174n
Shocker, Allan D., 72n
Simon, Herbert A., 35n, 131n
Skinner, Wickham, 83n
Slevin, Dennis P., 174n
Sproat, Audrey T., 131n
Staelin, Richard, 131n
Stevenson, Howard H., 112, 130n
Stewart, John M., 97n
Stobaugh, Robert B., 84n

Sultan, R. G. M., 83n, 107n
Summer, Charles E., 15n
Summers, G. F., 131n

Thomas, Philip S., 26, 35n, 131n
Thorelli, Hans B., 173n
Tod, Robert, 174n
Turoff, M., 147n

Vancil, Richard F., 34n
Vollmann, T. E., 84n
von Neumann, T., 145

Wasson, Chester R., 67
Wayne, K., 84n
Weinberg, Charles B., 131n
Weiner, D., 136, 146n
Weinhold, Wolf A., 15n, 173n

Wensley, Robin, 107n
Wheelwright, Steven C., 83n, 103, 104, 107n
White, George R., 97n
Wiersema, F. D., 107n
Wilson, Ian H., 137, 138
Woo, Carolyn Y. Y., 101, 107n
Wrapp, H. E., 15n
Wrigley, Leonard, 160

Yip, George S., 130n
Yuspeh, S., 70, 72n

Zaleznik, Abraham, 196n
Zeithaml, Carl P., 72n
Zennatos, Zenon S., 173n
Zentner, Rene D., 146n

SUBJECT INDEX

Acquisitions
   assimilation of, 169, 174*n*
   decisions on, 175*n*
   evaluation of, 168, 174*n*
   objectives in, 166, 171
Administration (*see* Management)
Administrative planning cycle, 32–33
Aerosol Techniques, Inc. (ATI), 92, 113
Air Products & Chemicals, Inc., 158, 173*n*
Airwick Industries, 164, 174*n*
Alignment, 15*n*
Allied Corporation, 182, 196*n*
Alternatives, 9, 11, 24
American Can Company, 43, 172, 175*n*
American Home Products, 14*n*
American Motors, 122
Antitrust, 131*n* (*see also* Regulation)
Attitude measurement, 131*n*
Autonomy, 160

Barriers to entry, 65, 130*n*, (*see also* Mobility barriers)
Bendix, 191, 196*n*
Beta coefficient, 173*n*
Boeing Company, 94, 97*n*
Boise Cascade Corporation, 183, 184

Brainstorming, 141
Break-even analysis, 75
Bristol-Myers Company, 120, 131*n*
"Bubble chart," 155
Business screening matrix, 45, 47
Business unit (*see* Strategic business unit)

Campbell Soup, 113, 114
Canadian Pacific Ltd., 120, 131*n*
Capacity expansion, 57
   and utilization levels, 80
CEO (chief executive officer), 187
Champion International, 190
Choice, 21, 24
Chrysler Corporation, 6, 15*n*
Ciba-Geigy Corporation, 164, 174*n*
Claimant analysis
   description of, 119
   framework of, 121
   structure of, 122
Club of Rome, 147*n*
CML Group, 174*n*
Coca-Cola Company, 164, 174*n*
Comparative advantage, 40
Competition (*see also* Rivalry)
   industry level, 115, 130
   reaction to, 29

Consistency, 4
COO (chief operating officer), 187
Corporate planning models (*see* Modeling)
Crises
    diagnostic framework for, 186
    operating, 185
    profit, 196
    strategic, 185
Cross-impact matrix, 139, 140
Cross-sectional analysis, 107n
Crown, Cork & Seal, 5, 14n, 43, 113, 130, 182, 196n
Culture, 196n

Data Resources, Inc., 137
Decentralization, 181
Decision making, 21, 24
Delphi process (*see* Environmental analysis)
Design & Manufacturing Company, 5, 14n, 81
Dialectic policy analysis, 143, 147n, 197n
Directional policy matrix (DPM), 161, 163, 173n
Distinctive competence, 40
Distribution systems, 71
Diversified (multibusiness) firms
    definition of, 181
    implications of, 152
    organizational responsibilities in, 160
Divestment, 166, 174n, 184
Divisionalization, 181
Dow Chemical, 66
duPont (E. I. duPont de Nemours & Company), 167, 174n

Easco, 50n
Economists, 118
Emerson Electric, 84n
Environmental analysis
    claimant analysis, 119
    Delphi process, 117, 140, 147n
    forecasting, 116, 136, 142
    role of in planning, 111
    scanning systems, 128

Environmental Protection Agency (EPA), 136
Environments
    constituencies in, 26
    general, 23
    internal, 23
    operating, 23
    as subsystems, 26
Esmark Company, 172, 175n
Evaluation criteria, 20, 171
Exit barriers, 72n, 115
Experience (learning) curve, 76
Exxon Corporation, 26

Federal Communications Commission (FCC), 25
Federal Trade Commission (FTC), 78
Financial analysis
    cash flow analysis, 60
    product line profitability assessment, 53
    tax analyses, 58
Forecasting (*see* Environmental analysis)
Formulation, strategy, 11
Freedom of Information Act (FOIA), 125, 131n
Frigidaire Division of General Motors, 94
Fuqua Industries, 27, 35n, 164, 174n
Futures research, 146n

Game theory, 145
General Electric Company, 45, 50n, 61n, 82, 91, 97n, 136, 137, 157, 173n, 188
General managers (*see* Strategic management)
General Motors, 97n
General Tire & Rubber Company, 173n
Goals of organizations
    concept of, 131n
    conflicting, 166
Goodyear Tire & Rubber Company, 158, 173n
Gould Corporation, 158
Growth-share matrix, 63, 154, 173n

Head Ski Company, 74
Hedblom, 93, 97n
Heublein, 160, 173n, 174n
Honeywell, 190
Human resource management (HRM), 97n

IBM Corporation, 122
Implementation, 12, 169, 179
Incentive systems, 21, 169, 191
Industrial dynamics, 147n
Industry sector
  analysis of, 113
  attractiveness of, 46
  competition within, 117
Inflation, 61n
Inland Steel Corporation, 165
Innovations, 22
Integrated (single business) firms
  evaluation criteria for, 19–20
  structural characteristics of, 19
Interdependency review chart, 105
Interdivisional matrix, 162
ITT, 16, 170, 174n, 184, 196n

Kennecott, 184
Kodak, 69

Leadership, 196n
Learning curve, 76
Litton Industries, 26
Logical incrementalism, 193
Logistics, 72n

Magic Chef, 94
Management
  characteristics of, 188
  efficiency of, 95
Manufacturing analysis
  capacity utilization analyses, 57, 80
  experience curve analysis, 76
  life cycles matrix, 104
  materials requirements planning (MRP), 82
  minimum efficient scale (MES), 79
Marketing analysis (see also Product life cycle)
  barriers to entry, 65, 130n
  share of market, 97n

Market segmentation, 64
Materials requirements planning (MRP), 82
Merger, 35n, 173n, 174n
Merrill Lynch, 94, 97n, 174n
Metagame analysis, 145
Middle management, 185
Minimum efficient scale (MES), illustrated, 79
Mission, 10
Mobility barriers, 48, 50n
Modeling, 107n, 147n
Motivational systems, 189
Multinational company (MNC), 131n

Negotiation framework, 124
Norton Company, 173n, 192, 196n

Objectives (see Goals of organizations)
Organizations
  complex, 5
  dimensions of, 19
  measurements and incentives of, 191

Pepsico, 164
Performance, 184
Philip Morris, 164
PIMS (profitability impact of marketing strategy)
  business unit comparisons with, 101
  general findings of, 100
  PAR reports of, 101
  research on, 72n
  and Strategic Planning Institute, 100
  strategy sensitivity reports of, 101
  use of, 100
Planning (see also Strategic planning)
  contingency, 135
  definition of, 4
Polaroid, 69
Policy, 3
Policy delphi, 142, 147n
Portfolio analysis
  for balance, 17, 155
  of incremental changes, 159
  of quantum changes, 159
Power, 13, 196n
PPG Industries, 123
Procter & Gamble Company, 164

Productivity, 97n
Product life cycle (PLC)
  concept of, 66, 107n
  multiproduct, 71
  planned, 70
  research on, 72n
Product/market position
  analysis of, 52, 73
  boundaries of, 72n
Programs, evaluation, 88

R&D (*see* Research and development)
Raadgvend Bureau Ir. B. W.
    Berenschot N.V., 98n
Raytheon, 94
Rationality, bounded, 28
Regulation, 27, 116, 130n
Research and development (R&D)
  components of strategy for, 85
  evaluation criteria and framework
      for, 87, 89, 92
  evaluation process for, 88, 91
  integrated planning framework for,
      103
  on processes, 86
  on products, 86
  timing of, 91
Return on investment (ROI)
  analysis of, 54, 90
  alternative calculations of, 59
  as incentive basis, 21
  PIMS use of, 100
Risk management, 17, 131n
Rivalry (*see also* Competition)
  industry sector, 115
  internal, 23
Rockwell International, 94
ROI (*see* Return on investment)

SBU (*see* Strategic business unit)
Scenarios, 136, 146n, 196n
SCM Corporation, 153
SDB, 133
Sears, Roebuck & Company, 5, 14n, 48
Sensitivity analysis, 55, 135
Shell Oil Company, 136, 173n, 196n
Simulation
  corporate, 143

functional area, 144
  world economy, 142
Singer Corporation, 153
Sony Corporation, 95, 97
SPS (*see* Strategic planning system)
Stakeholder analysis, 151 (*see also*
    Claimant analysis)
Standard Oil of Ohio, 157, 173n
Stanford Research Institute (SRI), 136
Stockholders, 27
Strategic analysis framework, 42
Strategic business unit (SBU)
  evaluation of, 180
  organizational level of, 30
Strategic choice, 3, 21
Strategic data base (SDB), 133
Strategic issues, 8
Strategic management, 23, 156
Strategic planning
  concepts of, 10
  definition of, 3
  framework for, 9
  introduction of, 3
  process of, 11, 24, 31, 180
Strategic Planning Institute (SPI), 100
Strategic planning system (SPS)
  administration of, 33
  definition of, 4
  development of, 193
  framework for, 12
  as two-cycle process, 194
Strategy
  alternative, 11
  definition of, 4
  elements of, 11
  levels of, 18
Strategy evaluation, 12
Strategy formulation, 11
Strategy implementation, 12
Synergy, 17, 175n
Systems dynamics, 145

Technology, 97n
Texas Instruments, 25, 35n, 84n, 193,
    194, 197n
Textron, 183, 196n
Time frames, 20
Timex Corporation, 74, 83n
Touche Ross, 97n

Trans World Corporation, 157
Trigger points, 135
Turnaround, 15n, 196n

Union Carbide Corporation, 158, 173n
Unionization, 94
UV Industries, 153

Value-added, 48
Values

managerial, 10
profile, 137, 138
Vulnerability analysis, 143, 144, 147n

Westinghouse Electric Corporation,
15n, 94
White Consolidated, 94, 97n
White Weld, 94

Xerox Corporation, 26